The Complete Guide to Tutoring Struggling Readers— Mapping Interventions to Purpose and CCSS

The Complete Guide to Tutoring Struggling Readers— Mapping Interventions to Purpose and CCSS

Peter J. Fisher
Ann Bates
Debra J. Gurvitz

Foreword by Darrell Morris

Teachers College, Columbia University
New York and London

The discussion in Chapter 6 on the Vocabulary Visit strategy draws on Blachowicz, C. Z., & Obrochta, C. (2006). Vocabulary Visits: Virtual Field Trips for Content Vocabulary Development. *The Reading Teacher, 59*(3), 262–268. Used with permission.

The discussion in Chapter 6 on PRC2 instructional design draws on Ogle, D., & Correa-Kovtun, A. (2010). Supporting English-Language Learners and Struggling Readers in Content Literacy with the "Partner Reading and Content, Too" Routine. *The Reading Teacher, 63*(7), 532–542. Used with permission.

Published by Teachers College Press, 1234 Amsterdam Avenue, New York, NY 10027

Library of Congress Cataloging-in-Publication Data

Fisher, Peter, 1948–
   The complete guide to tutoring struggling readers : mapping interventions to purpose and CCSS / Peter J. Fisher, Ann Bates, Debra J. Gurvitz.
      pages cm
   Includes bibliographical references and index.
   ISBN 978-0-8077-5494-8 (pbk. : alk. paper)
      1. Reading—Remedial teaching—United States.   2. Reading teachers— United States.   3. Tutors and tutoring—United States.   I. Bates, Ann, 1953–. II. Gurvitz, Debra J.   III. Title.
LB1050.5.F548 2013
372.43—dc23   2013031176

ISBN 978-0-8077-5494-8 (paper)
eISBN 978-0-8077-7247-8

Printed on acid-free paper
Manufactured in the United States of America

21   20   19   18   17   16   15   14   8   7   6   5   4   3   2   1

Contents

Foreword

For approximately 50 years (1925 to 1975), the university-based reading clinic was the major vehicle used for training our nation's reading teachers. Children who were struggling with reading would come to these clinics after school or during the summer, where they would be tutored, one-on-one, by a teacher-in-training. The tutoring was carefully supervised by a reading professor or one of his/her clinical staff. Everyone learned in these clinical practicums—the children, their tutors, even the supervisors who observed the lessons and provided guidance. Moreover, what was learned was sometimes shared with the wider reading community, including seminal ideas such as the informal reading inventory, the developmental spelling inventory, the directed reading-thinking activity (or DRTA), and the word sort approach to phonics instruction.

Although the clinical tradition in reading has waned over the past several decades, particularly at large research universities, it has remained alive and well at National Louis University, a Chicago-area school with a century-long commitment to quality teacher education. Peter J. Fisher, Ann Bates, and Debra J. Gurvitz, who each teach at National Louis, admirably carry forward the clinical torch in *The Complete Guide to Tutoring Struggling Readers*. Their book, which is comprehensive and well-written, addresses the issue of struggling readers within the context of our latest educational reform, the Common Core State Standards. It provides tutors and classroom teachers with valuable, well-organized information about how to help low-performing students in the areas of word recognition, fluency, comprehension, oral language, and writing. But what makes this book different is that one cannot read it without recognizing that the authors are writing from years of experience; they "have been there," they have tutored struggling readers themselves, and they have supervised the tutoring of others.

As an old reading clinician, I am impressed and gladdened that, in these changing times, Fisher, Bates, and Gurvitz take strong, consistent positions on three important issues. First, they acknowledge the critical role of *reading instructional level*: "Knowing the reading level or ability of a student is vital in order to match him to an appropriate-level text" (p. 2). The authors also adhere to the traditional instructional-level criterion of

95–97% for oral reading accuracy, a welcome confirmation in that it comes from university teachers who actually work with struggling readers.

Second, Fisher and his coauthors not only stress the significance of reading fluency (it frees the mind for comprehension), but they also point out that *reading rate* (i.e., pace or speed) can be a valuable measure of one aspect of reading fluency. Reading rate, because of the widespread use (or misuse) of the DIBELS oral reading fluency task in our schools, has become controversial in reading education circles. I believe that Fisher, Bates, and Gurvitz are correct in defending reading rate as an effective assessment measure *if* the rate score is obtained in a reading-for-meaning situation.

Finally, the authors argue throughout their book that *contextual reading practice*—at the correct level with interesting material—is by far the most important instructional activity. They write:

> The lesson components we emphasize also *reflect our belief that reading in connected text is the most valuable and useful activity that any reader can engage in.* No matter where the student is in terms of reading level or ability, most of the time [should be] spent in purposeful oral and silent reading. (p. 13, emphasis added)

Experienced reading teachers will recognize the truth value of the quote above. However, keep in mind the institutional pressure that is currently on primary-grade teachers to drill at-risk readers daily on phoneme awareness and nonsense-word decoding tasks, and to test and retest these skills every 2 weeks or so. How much time is taken up by these assessment-driven activities, and how much is left over for the contextual reading practice that the children sorely need? Or let us project forward a few years when elementary-grade teachers are required to conduct whole-class "close reading" lessons on difficult material (Common Core)—material that low-performing readers may be unable to read. Again, in these classrooms, how much contextual reading, at the correct level, will be done by low readers? These questions deserve our attention.

The Complete Guide to Tutoring Struggling Readers is an excellent book that is being released at the right time. The authors honor important ideas from the past while addressing the demands of the current educational context. For teachers who want to help struggling readers, this book will undoubtedly prove to be a valuable resource.

—Darrell Morris, Appalachian State University

Preface

This book is designed for those educators who want to plan and implement intervention lessons for struggling readers that align with the English Language Arts Common Core State Standards (ELA CCSS). It has been written by three educators who collectively have provided intervention for struggling readers at all grade levels in clinical and classroom settings, taught graduate-level clinical reading courses, and directed and supervised graduate students in reading improvement programs at urban and suburban sites. As educators we are committed and interested in helping teachers and tutors address the challenges they face in designing and implementing intervention lessons for students in primary, elementary, and middle schools.

In our reading intervention programs we use an instructional design that focuses on reflective practice to build students' independence in literacy that carries over from clinical settings to classrooms. We have learned from the graduate students enrolled in our programs that they value examples of explicit instructional and reflective practice revealed through case studies of struggling readers. What has evolved as a result is this book about teaching literacy that addresses how to design an intervention lesson across all grade levels, provides example tutoring plans and lessons, and describes procedures for teaching print skills, comprehension, vocabulary, fluency, and study skills.

The Common Core State Standards for the Language Arts provide an important reference point for working with all students. In relation to interventions, they provide meaningful standards that remind us as tutors and teachers what it is we are trying to accomplish with each reader and writer. In this text we try to relate practices which we have found promote literacy in struggling students to those standards. Any instructional practice may have multiple goals, and consequently, several standards may be addressed within one intervention lesson. Knowing this, as literacy educators, our overarching goal is to have students integrate their literacy practices in a way that addresses their purposes for reading. We view literacy as a tool for learning and, as such, strive to further students' reading and writing in ways that promote learning and the willingness and desire to learn.

This book is practical and reflects our work with students in various intervention settings. Each chapter ends with Things to Think About, and Further Resources for each chapter appear at the end of the book. Chapters 1 and 2 set the context. In Chapter 1 we introduce the framework for designing intervention lessons for struggling readers. We discuss the nature of motivation, reflective teaching and learning, and principles of tutoring. The focus is on key factors in acquiring optimal learning through the Gradual Release of Responsibility instructional model (Pearson & Gallagher, 1983), which shifts the learning from tutor to student, with the goal of building student independence and a transfer of learning from a one-on-one tutoring clinical setting toward independent classroom application. In Chapter 2 we take up components of the Intervention Lesson by featuring two case studies that address designing and implementing intervention plans with the goal of building independence. Additional examples show how tutors engage in diagnostic teaching.

Chapters 3 through 8 highlight literacy strategies, teaching suggestions, and materials, and provide the reader with a powerful set of instructional practices focused on specific interventions. Each chapter begins with a student profile representative of struggling readers enrolled in a reading improvement program and includes a matrix that matches focused intervention strategies to the English Language Arts Common Core State Standards, as well as sample lesson plans for the profiled students. Sidebars provide examples of how specific methods have been used with other students. The profiles and lesson plans vary in format and content reflecting the different difficulties students experience with literacy, and the many ways in which any particular difficulty may be addressed.

Chapter 3 addresses the development of print skills and word knowledge with younger readers. Chapter 4 looks at the development of contextual reading and fluency once students are beyond the initial stages of literacy. It also explores the selection of materials for young readers. Chapter 5 turns to developing students' knowledge of word meanings and ways to learn meaning from context. Chapter 6 stresses the importance of oral language in the development of literacy and how tutors can encourage conversations and discussions rather than gentle interrogations. Chapter 7 goes to the heart of reading—comprehension—and the issues of close reading and finding evidence for ideas and opinions. Finally, Chapter 8 suggests ways in which we develop writing in response to reading and make more explicit the connections between writing and reading. Finally, our conclusion reviews ideas which we consider important and worth revisiting. We also include a reference list of all the children's literature cited.

This book is written for future and current literacy teachers and tutors in the context of planning and implementing interventions for struggling readers. We have a combined experience of over 70 years of working with students who struggle with reading and writing. We know that each child is different, but we also know that the practices we recommend have been successful with many students over those years. We hope they will prove equally successful for you.

We would like to acknowledge Linne Elementary School and Christa McAuliffe Elementary School for housing summer reading programs. We thank all the colleagues who have worked with us in our summer programs, and who taught us as well as our students, in particular Betsy Niemiec, Carol Ivy, Eileen Owens, Laura Penn, Mary Kovats, MaryCaren D'Anniballe and Pana Kolintzas. Over the years Camille Blachowicz and Donna Ogle at National College of Education have supported and mentored us in our work: we could not have had better models and friends. *We are grateful to the Shaw Fund for Literacy for the continued support of our work and research with struggling readers.* Finally, we would like to acknowledge the support and perseverance of our editor, Jean Ward, who made it all come together in the end.

The Nature of Tutoring

When students enter a tutoring situation, they usually have experienced at least a year of failure in terms of literacy learning in school, leading to a negative self-concept as readers (Quirk, Schwanenfluegel, & Webb, 2009). These students have had difficulty in reading the assigned texts and also in writing in response to these texts. When students repeatedly experience failure and frustration, it is not surprising that many of them are unengaged or unmotivated when it comes to literacy. Part of the work of a tutor is to turn this situation around: to work in a way that motivates students to learn and to become engaged in their own learning. This book explores tutoring situations aimed at engaging students in literacy, and presents individual cases that exemplify struggling readers. Yet many of the instructional strategies we advocate are adaptable to small-group instruction and other instructional groupings, both within and outside classrooms.

It is commonly accepted that the experiences people bring to any situation influence how they think about it. For the last 25 years there has been great emphasis in literacy education on the use of background knowledge (or prior knowledge) in understanding and interpreting texts. At times this has led to too much emphasis on what the reader brings to a task and too little emphasis on what a text actually says. The ELA Common Core State Standards (CCSS) address this by asking students to engage with more complex texts, with complexity measured by three factors:

> *Qualitative evaluation of the text:* Levels of meaning, structure, language conventionality and clarity, and knowledge demands
> *Quantitative evaluation of the text:* Readability measures and other scores of text complexity
> *Matching reader to text and task:* Reader variables (such as motivation, knowledge, and experiences) and task variables (such as purpose and the complexity generated by the task assigned and the questions posed). (CCSS, p. 31)

In our experience, motivating a student to read is not merely a reader factor but, rather, part of the interplay among the reader, the text, and the task. A difficult task and a difficult text can make even the best of us unwilling to read and write. This chapter first explores the nature and nurture of motivation, and how it is impacted by reader, task, and text factors. Then we emphasize the importance of reflection on the tutoring session as it impacts subsequent sessions. Finally, we suggest four principles that underlie effective tutoring.

THE NATURE AND NURTURE OF MOTIVATION

Extrinsic motivation results from some external reward, such as grades or candy, for successfully completing a task. *Intrinsic motivation* is the reward of doing something for its own sake or because the individual thinks it is important in some way. A person will be intrinsically motivated to do something when two conditions are in place. First, the person must believe that accomplishing the task is possible. Second, the person must have the choice of engaging in the task. So, for students to be motivated to read and write, they need to believe that they *can* do it, and there needs to be some element of choice in what they are doing. Neither of these conditions is typically what they experience in a regular school setting, where extrinsic motivation in the form of grades or teacher praise is the norm.

Motivation is a complex construct, and educational psychologists have various theories that account for different aspects of how motivation works. For example, Guthrie and his colleagues have worked for many years in the area of motivation and literacy (Guthrie, Hoa, Wigfield, Tonks, Humenick, & Littles, 2007). Their construct of motivation includes students' interest in, attitude toward, and value placed on reading. Even though in theory these concepts can be discussed separately, in practice they are so intertwined and interrelated that trying to separate them does not help to increase students' motivation. Here, we will address motivation as part of the reader factors that can make a text complex, as defined by the ELA Common Core State Standards (CCSS).

Reader Factors

Reading level. Knowing the reading level or ability of students is vital, to be able to match them to an appropriate-level text. This book is not about diagnosis. It proceeds on the assumption that you will have some information about a student from school records, or from some form of testing. Once tutoring begins, you can change the level of text and the pedagogy through a process of diagnostic teaching—using your knowledge of literacy to modify instruction, as described in Chapter 2.

Interest. A student's interest in reading can be thought of in two main ways—as an interest in reading in general (or the value that the student places on reading), and an interest in reading situated in a specific context. Clearly, these two are very different and both have an impact on motivation. It could be argued that all interest is situated—that is, a student may place no value on reading in an academic context but may value reading in a social context. A student may value it in relation to a particular text (say, the current bestseller), but not in relation to a book of poetry. Reading may be valued as a way of obtaining a certain goal—reading enough books to reap a tangible reward—or devalued as a social stigma. There is also a sense in which reading can be valued as an activity to engage in for pleasure, in the same way that a person may watch television or go to the movies, and so may be valued in general. The issue for us, as teachers and tutors is how to generate enough enthusiasm through *situated interest* in reading and writing so that students will become more generally interested in literacy activities. That is, can you "turn students on to literacy" through your tutoring in such a way that they will not be turned off again when they are in regular classrooms without focused support?

Fortunately, you can develop a student's interest by making a given task interesting. In one summer program, an art teacher who was training as a reading specialist was struggling to motivate a 5th grader. After a few sessions of tutoring she brought in some of her architecture books, and for the rest of the summer she and her student read and wrote and built models about various forms of architecture. The student developed an amazing vocabulary, was empowered in ways that surprised him, and left the summer program feeling really good about himself and his literacy abilities. Who could have predicted he would be interested in architecture?

Engagement with text. What is engagement? If we think of motivation as a feeling that directs behavior toward certain goals (Maehr & Meyer, 1997), then we can see that it affects the initiation of and persistence in an activity, the level of intensity and involvement in an activity, and the attention paid and enjoyment derived from an activity. Each of these three ideas can be a part of engagement (Kolencik, 2010). Or perhaps it can be seen more easily in relation to students who are not engaged.

How can you know if students are not engaged? Do they stare into space? Do they constantly want to sharpen their pencils, go to the bathroom, or have other avoidance behaviors? Perhaps there are other students who constantly complain, "This is stupid" or "Do we have to read all of this?" Students like the latter may be suffering from *learned helplessness.* They have developed this defense of being pessimistic about everything to protect themselves from negative feedback or certain failure, because they are in a situation over which they have no control. Fear of failure also can lead to anxiety, which can cause withdrawal and nonparticipation. Why participate and risk looking like a fool in front of others? So there is no intensity and no involvement. The participation that does occur is forced and does not persist. There is a lack of attention and no enjoyment from the activity.

So how can students become engaged with text? The text has to be interesting and at the right level, and the reading has to be purposeful. This last idea tends to be neglected in relation to instruction. Adults rarely read unless it is purposeful. Even when reading for pleasure, adults know why they are reading. Too often in school, teachers do not set purposes for reading, or they set trivial purposes. For students to be interested and motivated to read, teachers need to provide *real* reasons to read (and write). Reading to learn about something that students are interested in does provide a purpose. It is up to you to generate an appropriate level of interest that can sustain motivation for purposeful reading, and one prerequisite is to provide interesting texts.

As with all constructs, we need to recognize that motivation is contextualized. That is, readers will be motivated to read in some situations. Even struggling adolescent readers may be comfortable "txtng" their friends. Perhaps what is most important to remember is that students are most likely to engage in an activity when they believe that successfully completing that activity depends on things they can control, such as their own effort, rather than luck or outside forces, such as teacher decisions that are perceived as arbitrary.

One primary area of concern in developing and maintaining students' interest in reading is to choose texts that are of interest to the students, and to engage them in tasks that they also find interesting. The texts do have to be on appropriate topics, and they also have to be at appropriate levels. This is crucial because we need to be working with them in their Zone of Proximal Development.

Task Factors

Zone of Proximal Development. Most educators are familiar with the concept of the Zone of Proximal Development. Russian social psychologist, Lev Vygotsky (1978), defined it as

> the distance between the actual developmental level as determined by independent problem solving and the level of potential development as determined through problem solving under adult guidance, or in collaboration with more capable peers. (p. 86)

More simply conceived, it is the difference between what the student can do cognitively with and without an adult's guidance. The zone is where the student is involved in the learning process and is actually learning. Too often in school, the teacher is doing all the work and the content of the lesson may be too hard for the students to understand. This is a vital concept in relation to tutoring. It is the tutor's responsibility to identify the student's Zone of Proximal Development so instruction will be at the appropriate level and, therefore, success will become likely and students will remain motivated and engaged.

Finding the Zones of Proximal Development for a student is part of diagnostic teaching. You will notice that we said "zones." That is because there will be different zones for the various components of reading and writing. A student may have print skills that enable him to decode text at a 6th-grade level, but he may struggle to understand 3rd-grade social studies, either because of vocabulary issues or because of comprehension-processing problems.

Similarly, a student may have excellent organizational abilities in her writing but struggle with spelling. As you begin tutoring with this student, think about how she is responding, and adapt your tutoring as you refine your understanding (or diagnosis) of her needs.

Tutoring is totally child-centered. In contrast to classroom teaching, where teachers may puzzle over how to differentiate classroom instruction to account for the needs of all their students, in tutoring there is the luxury of instructing at "just the right level." If the books or materials are too hard, or the task is too difficult, a student will become frustrated. As suggested above, students need to believe that they can complete a task successfully, so tutors need to design instruction that ensures that students will succeed. A central related concept is the gradual release of responsibility to the student.

Scaffolded instruction. If people cannot complete a task, they are grateful when someone helps. Similarly, students can be motivated if they are provided sufficient help in a way that enables them to gradually do more and more for themselves. This idea has been compared to a scaffold: Students should be provided as much scaffolding as needed to read successfully, and over time, more and more of the scaffold is taken away. Pearson and Gallagher (1983) discussed the gradual release of responsibility to the student (see Figure 1.1).

A tutor first demonstrates or models what she wants the student to learn, while the student watches. Some educators have called this stage, "I do, You watch." Then the tutor does it again but asks for the student's assistance—"I do, You help." Then the student tries, while the tutor provides

Figure 1.1. Gradual Release of Responsibility from Tutor to Student

	MODELING	**SHARED LEARNING**	**GUIDED PRACTICE**	**INDEPENDENT PRACTICE**
PEDAGOGY	*I do, you watch*	*I do, you help*	*You do, I help*	*You do, I watch*
Student involvement	Little or no control	Low control	Moderate control	High control
Tutor involvement	Modeling the process	Moderate support	Low support	Little or no support

the appropriate level of scaffolding—"You do, I help." Finally, the student does it independently—"You do. I watch." The time spent in each stage will depend on the process the student is learning and the speed at which the student learns. The gradual release of responsibility, then, is really about the level of scaffolding to provide—how much and when.

Task complexity. To us, hearing the phonemes (sounds) in a word seems simple. But to a child who does not even understand the word "boundaries," the task is actually complex. Tutors need to understand why a task seems complex to a student, and then try to make it less so. If a student cannot understand a passage that she can decode, what is the issue? Is it the length or difficulty of the sentences? Is it the vocabulary? Is it the organization of the text? Perhaps it is a combination of all three. Various literacy tasks require students to focus on different areas of a text. Writing a summary will require the student's understanding the main idea of a passage. Understanding character development asks the reader to look at characters' behavior, motivations, and emotions. You need to be aware then, of how the difficulty of the task—be it writing a summary, or retelling a story—is being impacted by difficulty in understanding specific components in a text.

Text Factors

A discussion of texts refers to all types of materials that you may use with readers in your tutoring, including magazines, journals, books, textbooks, and digital text. Three features of texts should concern us in terms of matching them to readers:

- *Surface features*, which include word and sentence difficulty and the length of the text
- *Content* of the text, which includes topic, genre, and organization
- *Formatting*, which includes typeface, spacing, and layout

Surface features. Most struggling readers have problems with words—either with word recognition/identification or with vocabulary, and usually a combination of both. Consequently, when matching a reader with a text, a primary consideration is the difficulty of the words that the reader will encounter. Interestingly, the decodability and the semantic difficulty of a word are related: Generally, the longer the word, the more difficult it is to read and to understand. For example, compare *home* and *domicile,* or *scold* and *castigate.* You can think of examples when this is not the case (e.g., *foyer* and *elephant*), but these are exceptions to a common relationship.

The second surface feature impacting on difficulty is the complexity of the sentences. Again, length is a shorthand measure of complexity, simply because the longer the sentence, the more subordinate clauses it will contain. However, merely shortening sentences does not necessarily make them more readable. "The dog ran away quickly when he saw the big hairy monster bare its fangs" is more readable than "The big hairy monster bared its fangs. The dog ran away quickly." In the first sentence the causal link is made specific, whereas in the latter case the link has to be inferred, so rewriting the sentence to make two shorter sentences does not actually make it more readable. Still, sentence length is a fairly good indicator of reading difficulty, especially if it is examined in "naturally occurring text." By this we mean text that has not been rewritten to reduce the readability as it might be measured by readability formulae.

Readability formulae can be used to find the difficulty level of a text. They all use some combination of word and sentence difficulty. Early attempts at measuring readability using formulae included many other factors, but ultimately none were found to contribute enough additional information to make them worth including in the measures. Many of the formulae are available online, and can be applied by typing segments of text into a word-processing program. As a caution: Make sure that the formulae you use are appropriate for the grade levels you are working with, and that you treat the results as just one component in your decision about which text to use with your student(s).

Most publishers of children's reading materials include reading levels for their materials. These levels may be the widely used: leveled books (Fountas & Pinnell, 2006), Reading Recovery (Reading Recovery Council of North America, 2004), the Developmental Reading Assessment (Beaver, 1997), lexiles (see www.lexile.com), or any of a number of others. One of the ways in which these leveling systems differ from readability formulae is the way they address difficulty by taking into account the familiarity of the content, the genre, and the layout (see discussion of format). You can find charts that attempt to equate the various leveling systems on the web, but as with readability formulae, you should select a level as just one component in your decisionmaking.

The final surface feature that you will want to consider is the length of the text. This will depend on the time frame in which you are tutoring. We strongly recommend that you use texts that you can complete in one or two sessions. Students who are, or have been, struggling with reading need a sense of accomplishment, so completing a reading task is important to them. Occasionally, younger students really want to read a "chapter book" because they have never done so before. In such instances, we find the shortest chapter book at the appropriate level that might interest them, so there is a good chance that it can be completed in a reasonable time frame. Then you might engage in some partner reading (with the tutor reading the longer of the two pages) to move through the book more swiftly. Fortunately, more and more materials are available in chapter book form for younger readers, so this task is easier than it once was.

Content. You want to find materials that will interest students in terms of content, but this has to be considered carefully in relation to who your students are and where and when you are tutoring them. Sometimes you have little choice and may have to try to find materials related to the school curriculum, but at the appropriate level of difficulty (see the discussion below about format). But students often have other interests on which you can build. The advantage of using students' existing knowledge is that they will bring an understanding of the vocabulary to the literacy task, and a willingness to learn new information. The reading and writing they undertake becomes purposeful when it adds to their knowledge and they can take ownership of the content, which allows you to focus on processes. To be interesting, texts have to be culturally relevant, so you should think carefully about the content of a text from the student's perspective.

Perhaps one characteristic typifies materials that interest students most: humor. Almost universally, humorous materials will engage students. Clearly, an unadulterated diet of such materials is not possible for all tutoring sessions, but a liberal sprinkling will help you and the student enjoy reading and writing together.

Publishers provide a great range of both fiction and nonfiction text at a variety of levels. In addition, the web is providing more and more opportunities for teachers to download good materials, and for students to interact with excellent digital text. Watching a brief videoclip also can stimulate interest in a topic. Some excellent magazines and trade materials are designed to interest students. In line with the recommendation about humorous content, there are several authors who write humorous poetry for children.

Format. Finally, the typeface, layout, and spacing of the materials will have an impact on the readability of the materials (and on interest level). The variety and size of type available to printers does not mean that all materials are now easier to read. Layouts are becoming more complicated. For adults raised on linear materials, the complexity and speed with which information is presented in the digital age can be mind-blowing. In Chapter 7, when addressing comprehension, the "new literacies" are discussed in relation to issues raised by modern technology. In terms of interest, digital materials clearly can be motivating for some students simply because of their novelty. Still, not every student has access to the Internet at home, and those who need tutoring are more likely to be among the ones who do not have such access.

THE TUTOR AS REFLECTIVE TEACHER

Tutoring is a luxury that most teachers do not have. It is a luxury in the sense that a tutor has the opportunity to spend an extended time examining the literacy processes of students who are struggling with reading and writing, and to begin to understand how those processes operate, not just for these students but also for many students in your classroom and school. To take full advantage of this opportunity, you will have to engage in reflective teaching. You will have to consider whether you are implementing instruction appropriately, whether the text is a good one for the task, and how the instruction is impacting on the student.

In diagnostic teaching, assessment and teaching are interactive and ongoing processes. Observing students' responses to teaching allows you to evaluate a student's developing knowledge and understanding of literacy processes, and to adapt instruction accordingly. For example, if a student misreads *phone,* you may know that the long 'o' is not a particular area of concern and that the student has read *stone* correctly, and suggest a strategy: "Can you think of a word that ends the same way?" Or adapting instruction may take a more conscious form of rethinking a lesson for the next tutoring session, because this is the third long-'o' pattern that the student has missed in his reading.

Although tutoring can be an exciting and energizing exploration of how students learn and how they have difficulties with learning, it can also be exasperating when students are not learning and the explanation is not readily available. Our combined experience of more than 50 years in running tutoring programs leads us to believe that, when tutors and students work together to address literacy issues, students will have success and— perhaps for the first time—begin to enjoy reading and writing.

PRINCIPLES OF TUTORING

Often, there is no obvious reason why a tutoring session is or is not successful. However, certain principles seem to be conducive to success.

Listen to the Student

No teaching situation is more student-centered than tutoring. For students, tutoring offers a rare opportunity to receive focused attention from a knowledgeable and caring adult, and a time when someone actually may listen to what they have to say. Some tutors are surprised that students are self-aware about what they can and cannot do in relation to reading and writing. Of course, not all students do know this, and one of your goals of tutoring should be to get them to be more metacognitive about their own learning. One certainty is that tutoring is more successful when you ask a student whether she understands, and whether what you are doing makes sense to her. A student may give you useful information in other ways, too, such as talking about what a teacher has done successfully. If you listen carefully, you can avoid teaching something that a student already knows how to do, or a strategy that has not worked for him in the past.

Collaborate with the Student

Students should be involved in their own learning. Too often, students who need tutoring have never been asked to take control of their own learning, and may even think that they are missing some magic element—if only someone would tell them what it is. Also, you should avoid the use of unnecessary authority. A student has to trust you. You can be an authority figure, but none of the decisions can appear arbitrary or unreasonable. Tutoring should be a place where students feel like participants and do have at least some control over what happens. Therefore, unless there is some reason for not doing so (such as an early intervention framework), give students some choice as to the order in which they engage in the activities in a tutoring session—a small but effective way of making them feel in control.

Maintain an Appropriate Pace

You have to keep a session moving so you can provide the maximum instruction in the time allowed. At the same time, you have to allow space for a student to learn. This has to be balanced with good pacing, but too often tutors are anxious to fill a silence with an extra prompt or suggestion—and end up doing all the talking. As one tutor put it, "Students learn in the space of our supportive silence." We are not sure that is always the case, but we think the spirit is correct: you have to allow time for students to process, think, and take control of their own learning. This gradual release of responsibility means that students need time to practice what you have taught them. Sometimes you may think you should be doing *something* when watching a student practice what you have taught, and yet, just being available to help if needed may be as important as "teaching" something in the first place.

Plan Effectively

Often, tutors overplan. You might expect students to do more than they can actually accomplish in the allotted time. This is not necessarily a bad thing. It is better to overplan than to underplan. Too much overplanning, however, is a waste of time and energy. Effective planning occurs when you understand a student's needs and know some ways of meeting them effectively. The sample lesson plans in subsequent chapters can be adapted to meet the learning needs of your students.

In this book you will find information to become a successful tutor who engages in effective diagnostic teaching of reading and writing. The goal is to develop your understanding of literacy pedagogy as it applies to struggling readers. Much of what we write about is adapted from classroom instruction or can be adapted for classroom instruction. Much has also been said before in different ways and in different forums. We hope that the way we have put it together here will make sense for you in your situation with your students.

Things to Think About

1. What motivates you to do something? How is it related to your interest in doing it —specifically and in general?
2. From your experience, think of a good student, an average student, and a poor student who were not engaged in a school task. Can you speculate as to why?
3. When you choose a book, what criteria influence your decision? How does purpose impact on your decisionmaking? Can you recall what influenced you when you were a child?

2 The Intervention Lesson and Diagnostic Teaching

Teachers know that the success of a lesson usually depends on careful preparation. In the case of tutoring, this becomes even more important, and can be time-consuming, because the lesson needs to address the specific needs of the students and do so in their zones of proximal development. We have found that having a basic framework for an intervention lesson for a particular student allows for consistency across lessons and reduces the time that tutors need to prepare. As tutors in our programs often tell us, "I didn't know that preparing for one student could take so much work."

The importance of thoughtful planning is matched by the necessity for thorough record-keeping. This includes notes added to the written lesson plan that describe what actually occurred: the activities completed, anecdotal notes on the student's responses and reading behaviors, and scores from ongoing formative assessments such as running records and fluency measures. Gains in the student's reading level, your ultimate goal, are not just duly recorded but are celebrated with the student and communicated to parents and classroom teachers. Careful record-keeping is essential for planning the next lesson and for holding you accountable for your work. In the lesson templates included at the end of each chapter, the third column, entitled "Outcomes and Formative Assessments," provides space for you to annotate during the lesson.

COMPONENTS OF AN INTERVENTION LESSON

How you spend your time with your students and what components you choose to include in your lessons represent what you believe the child needs to become a more successful, engaged reader and what you believe in and value in terms of reading development and instruction. For example few readers, including proficient adult readers, would not benefit from increasing their vocabularies or developing strategies to improve their reading comprehension. In contrast, not all readers need to increase their reading rate or work on decoding one-syllable words. So certain lesson components should be part of almost any intervention lesson, such as a comprehension activity, and some components may be included on an as-needed basis, such as working to improve decoding or reading rate.

Further, you must choose lesson components judiciously, recognizing that time is your currency: You need to make good use of every minute that you have with students in the tutoring setting. This may be the only instructional time when lessons are designed to meet a child's specific, individual needs, and may indeed be the only time when text difficulty is carefully selected to meet the student's current reading capabilities. Troubling evidence suggests that students who struggle in reading spend little time actually reading. Allington (2002) found that there was only 10–15 minutes of actual reading in a typical 90-minute reading block, and in many classrooms students read for only 20 minutes during the school day. We don't think that things have changed a great deal since that study was published. This lack of constructive practice is a significant contributor to many students' ongoing problems with literacy.

The four areas of concern in reading diagnosis—print, vocabulary, comprehension, and fluency—should all be considered in planning the intervention lesson. Presumably, one or more of these areas has been identified as a main concern for the student, and this would be reflected in components of the intervention lesson. This is not a matter of necessarily leaving out anything, but more a matter of emphasis and time allotment.

The lesson components we emphasize also reflect our belief that reading in connected text is the most valuable and useful activity that any reader can engage in. No matter where a student is in terms of reading level or ability, most of the student's time is spent in purposeful oral and silent reading. We see tutoring as an opportunity to pay off some of the debt that many of these students have accumulated in terms of print exposure. Many students who struggle with reading have had few opportunities to do what they actually need most: to read connected text successfully. So even when students demonstrate the need for work in print skills at the word level, we believe that, after providing some short, focused instruction in an activity such as word sorting or word building, this is best applied and practiced through contextual reading.

Another consideration must be the order of events, or how the lesson will unfold. For some students, this order will be important to the actual teaching. For other students it will be less important, and indeed can be negotiated with the student.

Finally, the grade level of students is an important consideration in lesson planning. Younger students are learning to master the print system while attending to story elements and other information. To capture and maintain their attention, you will need to spend less time on each component of the lesson. Older readers might need to build more sustained attention to reading to develop the stamina for spending extended time with text. Middle school and high school students may also need, as part of their vocabulary and comprehension work, study skills to help them navigate and use their content-area textbooks.

The utility, or usefulness, of an activity within a lesson component also has to be considered. You can be overwhelmed by the number of activities and teaching strategies you know and value, and would like to use with your students. We believe that your time is best spent on approaches that have the best chance of transference to the independent reading or studying situation. The question to ask is, "Can the student learn to use this without my support?" This criterion helps you narrow the choices, allowing you to focus on those strategies that have some currency away from the support setting. This is what tutoring instruction must eventually enable the student to do.

An example of a comprehension strategy that has high utility away from the teacher or tutor is visualization. Teaching students to use mental images or to "make a picture in your mind" is something they can then do on their own as the need arises. You can identify when readers may find this strategy useful and practice doing it with students. In contrast, constructing a story map is not something that readers are likely to initiate as a comprehension strategy when reading independently.

The other criterion to keep in mind when choosing among teaching strategies or instructional activities is the authenticity of the act. Is this something readers really do in order to read, understand, and respond to text? It helps to think about what proficient readers, who choose reading over other competing activities, do to maximize their literary experiences: discuss a book or article with other readers or with significant people in their lives, read a review of a book, or search for other works by that author. Some of these authentic responses highlight the social aspects of reading—the satisfaction from engaging with others around literacy acts. Examples of reading response activities that do not meet this standard for authenticity include things like writing a new ending to a story or answering "gotcha"-type questions about insignificant details. Such probes suggest, and are designed to reveal, a reader's lack of recall of minutia. This line of questioning would not make one popular in a book club of adult readers!

In this chapter we will first address lesson components by sharing some actual cases at different grade levels where tutors designed lessons using components that met the students' needs and represented sound reading instruction in general. We will consider the nature of the activities that seem to work best in each area of reading. What kinds of reading activities lend themselves well to the intervention lesson? We have found, for example, that partnering activities work well, because these allow for the tutor and the student to work together in a reciprocal manner—giving you the opportunity to provide ongoing modeling, helping with the pace of the lesson, and giving the student a "break" from being accountable for every item and response. Keep in mind that the intensity of a one-on-one lesson can be tiring, so you sometimes must assume the role that a more capable peer might in a classroom setting. The second part of the chapter explains diagnostic teaching as a way to learn what students can and cannot do and provides examples of the decision making that is a part of such teaching.

And we can't say it enough: We believe that every reader improves by reading more. Quantity is important! Notice that the reading of connected, authentic text is the primary component in our lessons.

THE EARLY INTERVENTION LESSON, GRADES K–1: SUSAN

Early intervention to prevent reading underachievement has been an area of study for decades, and many lesson formats have been offered. Many of these are based on the work of Marie Clay's Reading Recovery model (Clay, 1993). Because that specific program cannot be replicated outside of a licensed Reading Recovery site, it is not useful or responsible to discuss that format here but, rather, to present those lesson formats that have been derived successfully or in the spirit of those intervention principles. In general, these include:

1. The reading of familiar text
2. Ongoing assessment using a running record
3. Word work
4. Writing to develop print skills
5. Guided reading in a new text

In summer reading programs such as ours, there is often the luxury of a 1-hour lesson. This is unrealistic in schools, as is the opportunity to work with children one-on-one. The 30-minute lesson is more common, and this usually includes two or more students in an intervention group. We will present a lesson format here that is designed for a 30-minute, one-on-one lesson for early readers who are at risk or who have fallen behind already. These children need a steady, dependable program that is delivered with frequency. Daily is ideal and will yield the best results. It is better to meet with a young child more frequently for less time than it is to meet less frequently for more time—so a well-structured 30-minute lesson three times a week is better than a 1-hour lesson once or twice a week.

We have chosen Susan as an example of an intervention lesson. She ended 1st-grade reading at a beginning 1st-grade, or preprimer, level. Initial testing showed that she attempted to read for meaning. She recognized when an error had been made but was unable to do much to help herself; her sight vocabulary appeared to be very limited, and she was not using letter-sound knowledge beyond the initial letter cue to solve new, unfamiliar words. This also was demonstrated in her developmental spelling, in which she was secure in representing the initial letter, but not with ending or medial sounds.

Instructional Plan for Susan

Susan's tutor decided to work to develop her print skills using a variety of engaging word study activities, while also immersing her in reading text at her instructional level. In each of these lesson components, the tutor provided levels of support designed to gradually recede, allowing Susan to become independent and successful. Her tutor developed the following instructional plan for Susan:

- Contextual reading at Susan's current instruction level, PP2 (level D, Fountas and Pinnell, 2006); with rapid advancement to primer level (H), where the number of trade books available increases. Supportive methods, such as echo and partner reading, will be used to introduce new books; repeated readings to increase exposure to words and develop fluency.
- Introduction of trade books and informational text for reading by the student and for tutor read-alouds (at higher text levels) to build background knowledge and conceptual vocabulary.
- Development of sight vocabulary of 200 words, emphasis on frequency and reliable spelling patterns being used in the word study portion of lesson. Word bank, word sorting, and word building activities will be used.
- To develop comprehension skills, the DRTA (Directed Reading-Thinking Activity will be used during guided reading, and DLTA (Directed Listening-Thinking Activity) used during read-alouds. Stopping points will be marked for Susan to make predictions.
- Writing for sound and to create original, meaningful sentences that can be used for rereading, word for the word ring, and short lessons based on letter-sounds relationships, spelling patterns, and writing conventions such as capitalization and punctuation. These will be based on what Susan demonstrates in her writing.

The lesson plan format presented in Figure 2.1 was developed by Darrell Morris (2008) for his Early Steps intervention program. We have

Figure 2.1. Lesson Plan for Susan

Student: Susan

Session 4

Lesson Component	Strategies and Activities	Outcomes and Formative Assessment
Rereading Familiar Text **Title:** *Kitten Chased a Fly,* Beverly Randall, 1998 **Level:** C	**Words:** *away, got*	Susan identified both words (*away, got*); in text. Accurate reading; ready to try level D.
Running Record **Title:** *I Can Jump,* Joy Cowley, 1986 **Level:** C	**Goal:** 95% accuracy	**Accuracy:** 98% She has maintained accuracy above 95% in six Level C books; move to Level D
Word Study	**Word Bank** Review cards and word ring **Word Sort:** rhyming short a families: mad tap can glad snap ran Dad nap plan pad trap than **Spell Check:** mad, trap, ran, than, nap	**Word Bank:** Added *jump, like,* came to her word ring Put *got, away* on cards **Spell check:** tan/than tarp/trap She needs work with blends, digraphs
Writing for Print Skill Development	**Sentence:** Susan writes her own sentence about her pet hamster.	**Sentence:** My hamster got out, but I found him. **Focus:** Encoded to add *t* in hamster; *ou* as in *out*.
Guided Reading: New Book **Title:** *The Horrible Big Black Bug,* Toni Jacquier, 1984 **Level:** D	**Introduction:** Preview text Echo read Independent read	Following preview, we were able to partner read; then Susan read independently. Preview may have revealed too much; make sure there are words for her to solve.

had success with this plan in our reading programs, as well as in an after-school tutoring center that we have co-sponsored for more than 30 years. Once a student reaches primer-level text (mid-1st grade), Morris suggests matching the student with another reader and modifying the lesson for two students, alternating days for the running record, taking turns in sorting, and so forth.

Description of the Lesson

Rereading familiar text. Notice that Susan's plan begins with her rereading of familiar text—little books she has read in the previous day or two. This activity is important for Susan, and so is its placement at the beginning of the lesson. Her tutor wants Susan to begin the lesson in a positive way, doing something they both know she can do successfully. This is comforting and empowering for Susan, who, before this intervention program began, had few experiences that made her feel like a reader.

From the tutor's perspective, the benefits of rereading familiar text are enormous, too, because his primary goal for Susan at this point is to build a sight vocabulary of about 200 words that Susan recognizes instantly and without conscious analysis. The daily repeated reading increases Susan's exposure to the essential words she needs to be able to move ahead in text level, and thereby catch up to her peers.

Running record. One of the books Susan is rereading is a book previewed and read the day before: A running record is taken so that her tutor can confirm, by Susan's accuracy, that this book is appropriate for instruction-level reading.

Word study. Another lesson component that addresses the goal of word recognition is word study. One activity is a *word bank.* Susan's tutor has targeted certain high-frequency words for Susan to learn in each book, and these are "spot-checked" following each reading: He points to the word in a sentence and asks Susan to read it. The words she can identify in this manner are written on cards. The cards are then stored in an envelope—colorfully decorated by Susan and labeled "Susan's Words." The words for the story "*Kitten Chased a Fly*" (Randall, 1998) are the high-frequency words *away* and *got,* and these are added to the cards in the envelope. Each day, her tutor goes through all of the cards in the envelope with Susan. When she reads a word correctly, a check is placed on the back of the card. After three checks, the card is placed on a word ring. The word ring words are reviewed weekly. We have noticed that this specific lesson component quickly becomes the children's favorite, and it is easy to see why: they see, in a quantitative way, the progress being made. It is represented for them in this growing collection of words.

Within the Word Study lesson component, which addresses the need for the early reader to identify words accurately and quickly, Susan's tutor engages her in activities such as *word sorting* and *word building*. These are designed to have her discover, through analysis and manipulation of letters, some common, reliable spelling patterns that will help her to decode new words she encounters in text. In this lesson, Susan is sorting short "a" rhyming word "families." The procedures for this activity, Word Sorting, and for Making Words, which is also used for the Word Study component of the lesson, are described in detail in Chapter 3.

We would like to emphasize here that the Word Study portion of the lesson, while providing powerful and essential instruction and practice, should not take more than 5–10 minutes of the lesson. We have noticed that this time frame is difficult to adhere to for many tutors, either because they are learning to manage their time or because they believe that the child's needs indicate that the child will benefit from more time spent on these activities. We believe that a well-designed word study lesson, where the child is doing all of the work, is short but rigorous—and it allows for more time spent in contextual reading, where the child has the opportunity to apply, in real text, what she is learning about words.

Writing for print skill development. The writing portion of this early intervention lesson usually involves the construction of one sentence. It serves the purpose of developing and securing the child's understanding of letter-sound relationships, concept of word, and word identification. The sentence is either offered by the student or dictated by the tutor. The student writes the sentence with some tutor support: for prompting the child to stretch out sounds for spelling, to consult the child's word bank or word wall to spell irregular high-frequency words, to remind the child to apply writing conventions such as capitalization and punctuation, and to fully spell for the child those words she cannot yet access through her current print knowledge. The completed sentence is read, and one feature from it used for a quick, "teachable moment" mini-lesson.

Susan offered the following sentence:

My hamster got out but I found him.

Susan is able to write the words *my, got, out, but,* and *him* accurately on her own, using her own letter-sound knowledge or by referencing her word bank. Her tutor helps her with the word *hamster:* The first syllable Susan could write by segmenting the sounds herself, the second half her tutor supplies for her, but with just a mention about the sound for 'er,' because she has not yet learned that combination. Her tutor chooses to help Susan with the "ou" combination in *found,* pointing out that it is the same sound she just wrote in *out.*

Guided reading. In the New Book portion of the lesson, Susan is supported through her first encounter with a text. The plan shows that her tutor intends to begin with an introduction of the text, where he will purposefully use some new vocabulary as he previews each page. This will be followed by echo or partner reading, where he and Susan take turns reading. Finally, Susan will read the book on her own. The same text will be used the following day for the running record, and as a familiar, easy read on the third day.

INTERVENTION LESSON, GRADES 2–5: PAUL

Once struggling readers get beyond the initial stages of reading development, their needs become more complex. It usually is no longer just an issue of developing print skills (although that can be a large part), but of addressing issues of comprehension, vocabulary, and fluency. Whereas learning print skills is a matter of mastery, there are no specific ways of "mastering" comprehension, as it is so complex. Similarly, each student's vocabulary knowledge is unique, so what is addressed, and how, can vary greatly. In neither instance is there a developmental process that can be followed in the same way that it can be addressed in print skill work. The structure of the intervention lesson, therefore, can vary from student to student. Often there are similar components, but the amount of time spent on each component, and how reading and writing are addressed within them, may be very different. In the following sample intervention lesson we provide a framework that can be adapted and changed. Normally the components include:

- Word study—recognition, identification, spelling
- Comprehension
- Word study—meaning
- Fluency
- Writing

A further difference from an early intervention lesson is that each of these need not be addressed in every session, and that the time spent on each may vary. Also, work with a given text may continue across several sessions.

We have chosen Paul as an example of an intervention lesson for grades 2–5. Paul is an entering 3rd-grade student who has had difficulty with reading ever since his first experiences with formal instruction in kindergarten. His instructional reading level is late 1st-grade; his independent level, where he can read on his own without support, is primer, or mid-1st-grade level. Paul is able to read words in isolation but has difficulty with these same words in contextual reading. Paul's persistent attempts to fix his reading errors (he is quite good at monitoring his reading) results in a very slow reading rate. His low accuracy and overall dysfluency are reflected in his incorrect or lack of responses to factual or detail-oriented questions following oral and silent reading. He is more successful with higher-level questions that require inference and evaluation or vocabulary knowledge.

Instructional Plan for Paul

Paul's tutor realized at once the challenge she would face in finding materials for him, given the gap between the text complexity he could manage and his age and grade level. In the time she had spent testing Paul and getting to know him, one thing was evident aside from his difficulty with integrating print cues: He was a very bright student who had extensive experiences that would be useful in academic work. How could she expect him to be motivated by a text written for a 1st-grade student? Paul had indicated that he liked reading nonfiction—sports stories and anything funny. With all of this information in mind, she developed the following instructional plan:

- Guided reading at Paul's instructional reading level, late 1st-grade, with a focus on accuracy and attention to important details; Predicting using the DRTA to support inferential thinking
- Word study to improve Paul's word recognition skills and build his sight vocabulary; Word sorting and word building to highlight vowel patterns; A word bank or word wall for use as a reference for spelling
- Repeated reading in familiar text to improve all facets of fluency: accuracy, rate, phrasing, expression, and prosody; Humorous poetry and favorite passages can be used to make this practice authentic and enjoyable
- Writing for different purposes: to share information, to respond to reading, to express ideas
- Read alouds by the tutor, with a comprehension strategy modeled and practiced, to provide Paul with the opportunity to hear and discuss material at a level more consistent with his grade and interests

See the sample lesson plan for Paul in Figure 2.2, which is designed as Lesson 8.

Figure 2.2. Lesson Plan for Paul

Student: Paul

Lesson 8

Lesson Component	Strategies and Activities	Outcomes and Formative Assessment
Independent level text/repeated reading: *The Baseball Game,* Helen Depree, 1997 **Level:** I	Bar graph accuracy and rate over three readings. Compare with previous graphs.	Rate is improving: 42, 51, 68 wpm; accuracy 92, 94, 97%. Paul sees his progress and is taking more responsibility for completing the graphs.
Running record: *Fox on the Job,* James Marshall, 1988, Ch.1 **Level:** J	Aiming for 90+% accuracy–review miscues	96% significant accuracy: *Week/wreck:* Paul did not self-correct or stop at this significant error. Discussed the silent *w* in this word. Adds and deletes words that are not significant errors: grammatically correct and not disruptive to meaning.
Word study: Making words *"ea"* letter pattern as a focus	**Mystery word:** *catcher* at hat hate rate rat crate ate eat tea teach cheat chat cat catch catcher	Sequencing letters is still difficult. This is better for him than sorting; may help him more with spelling. He chose *catch* and *teach* for his word ring.
Guided reading: *Fox on the Job,* James Marshall, 1988, Ch. 2–3 **Level:** J	Use Questioning the Author queries to prompt retelling of story events: "What just happened?" "What is the author telling us about this character?"	Paul enjoys this character and delights in his imperfections. Could introduce Character Map with this series.
Writing: Edit, proofread baseball story	Use of post-its as a flag for proofreading errors	Paul finds his errors in capitalization and punctuation; needs probes to find spelling errors. Make a word wall of irregular, high-frequency words for reference.
Read aloud: *Treasure Island,* R. L. Stevenson (graphic novel), 2006	During the read aloud model the comprehension strategies of rereading to clarify and summarizing. At the end Paul will dictate a summary to add to his previous work.	My rereading frustrates him a bit; he is impatient and eager to move ahead in the story. Continue to model and practice this; he needs this for his summary.

Description of the Lesson

Repeated reading. Paul enjoys the repeated reading activity, where he graphs his time reading a short passage and the number of errors in three consecutive readings. Paul knows that increasing oral accuracy and rate are two of his reading goals, and he works on both in this activity, cheerfully competing against himself in each trial. His tutor likes starting with this, too, because it engages Paul and provides a reading "warm up." The simple bar graph, which Paul colors in, is a record of progress that he can see and understand. His tutor also uses questions and probes following each reading to demonstrate to Paul how much more he is able to recall and understand with each reading. He is beginning to recognize, and can articulate, the value of practicing and the benefits of rereading—a strategy he can use on his own as needed.

Running record. A running record is used daily to check Paul's accuracy in a text he read the previous day in guided reading. His tutor is interested in how much Paul has retained from the previous session, and whether he is ready to move to the next text level. She keeps a log of his book titles, the levels, and his daily accuracy scores.

Word study. Paul's word study activity for this lesson is one of his favorites—Making Words (Cunningham, Hall, & Heggie, 2001b)—a word building activity in which Paul uses letter-sound relationships and long- and short-vowel spelling patterns to construct and deconstruct words, eventually leading to the discovery of the "mystery" word, which uses all of the letters available. His tutor selected a meaningful word around the theme of baseball—*catcher*—and developed a series of prompts that asked Paul to build words containing the spelling features he needed to practice. She prompted him:

- Make the word *at*
- Add a letter to make *hat*
- Add letter to make *hate*
- Change a letter to make *rate*
- Add a letter to make *crate*

This continued with prompts that completed the following word sequence that his tutor prepared in advance:

at hat hate rate rat crate ate eat tea teach cheat chat cat catch catcher

Paul loves the game-like features of this activity, and his tutor sees the workout he is getting in sequencing the letters correctly to match sounds and in remembering the vowel patterns that contain silent letters. This activity is not easy for Paul, nor should it be. He is working in his Zone of Proximal Development, doing the work under his tutor's guidance. He is motivated to solve the mystery word, which he did in this instance.

To make the most of the activity, his tutor wrote the words on cards and showed these to Paul to check for instant recognition. He then chose two for his word ring, *teach* and *catch*. The word *cards* can also be used for an open sort, where the student categorizes them according to features he notices (Cunningham, Hall, & Heggie, 2001b). This is certainly an option if the tutor thinks it will be helpful with that particular set of words.

Guided reading. Paul reads Chapters 2 and 3 of *Fox on the Job* by Edward Marshall (1988) for the guided reading portion of the lesson. This series is a hit with Paul, who needs exactly what these books provide: accessible print with, by comparison, higher levels of literary elements (humor, characterization, and plot). His tutor uses open-ended queries that allow Paul to retell story events, discuss character traits, and make predictions. This is an example of how his tutor masterfully uses one of Paul's strengths—inferential thinking—to target an area of need—retelling.

Writing. Paul's writing activity for this lesson involves editing a piece he was working on for the program's Summer Writers, a collection of student writing that was published weekly. Because an actual reading audience of fellow students and family members see this, Paul understands that he must follow writing and spelling convention in his final version. His tutor uses a method for guiding students through this editing process that allows her to support Paul while giving him as much independence as possible. First, she invites him to read the piece aloud and find and correct what he notices himself. Next, she attaches a sticky flag to each line where there was something additional that needs to be fixed (adding a number to the flag if there was more than one edit to make in a line), and then gives Paul the chance to find and make the corrections on his own. Nearly all of the necessary edits are completed in these two steps. The few remaining steps are those that Paul is not able to see or fix on his own, even with prompting. His tutor helps him with these (spelling of scoreboard and division), modeling how she chunks and divides longer words for spelling and analysis.

Read-alouds. There is time for a read-aloud at the end of this lesson, and she continues with *Treasure Island* (Stevenson, 2006), a graphic novel that Paul has selected. She does most of the reading here, as the novel is difficult for Paul at the print level. Still, there are parts he can read, and she invites him to do so when appropriate. For comprehension, she targets summarizing, and leaves time at the end of the lesson for Paul to dictate a short summary of the day's story events. This is added to his previous summaries of *Treasure Island,* eventually creating a full summary of the novel. This portion of the lesson gives Paul the opportunity to work at a higher conceptual level than his current print skills would allow.

Follow-up. The lesson ends with Paul taking the *Treasure Island* book home to reread with his father. The graphic novel helps to bridge the difference between Paul's reading and interest levels, and the classic nature of the book assures Paul's father that he was being exposed to challenging material. Further, because Paul heard the story read aloud by his tutor earlier in the day, it is possible for him to partner-read portions of it with his father. This is a time they both enjoy and look forward to.

INTERVENTION LESSONS, MIDDLE SCHOOL

Middle school students may still have print skill and comprehension issues, but they have to work primarily with expository text in the content areas, and their school work primarily concerns learning from various texts in both paper and digital forms. In addition, content-area studies place an additional emphasis on learning and applying academic vocabulary, and on writing to demonstrate learning. Vocabulary learning can often be linked with print skill instruction because students at this level frequently benefit from morphology instruction, which can be helpful in word identification, spelling, and word meaning. So, in addition to dealing with comprehension issues, tutors often need to work on studying, vocabulary knowledge, and writing. As with elementary-grade students, there is considerable variability in what middle school students need, but a typical intervention lesson might include:

- Comprehension
- Word study—meaning and identification
- Studying
- Writing

Students at this level often deal with quite complex texts, so instruction with a specific text—or writing to demonstrate learning of a specific topic—may extend across several sessions. The plans may look similar to Paul's, but activities from Chapter 7 (comprehension instruction) may play a greater role.

We believe that students become readers through multiple routes, and no one reader may get there in exactly the same way as another reader

Perhaps the hardest thing to do as a tutor is to recognize when something is not working, and that a student may be processing words or texts in ways we had not thought of. You need to adjust instruction in every session to fit a student's needs and accomplishments. Sometimes this is called diagnostic teaching, which we discuss next.

DIAGNOSTIC TEACHING

As a tutor, you may come to the instructional situation knowing little more than some test results provided by the school, and a parent's comments, such as, "She has a hard time reading the words." A reading specialist may conduct further tests to determine exactly what a student can and cannot do, but you may need to make these decisions as you teach a student. Diagnostic teaching means examining what a student can do during and as a result of instruction, and thinking about what it tells you about a student's reading and writing abilities, what requires addressing, and modifying instruction appropriately. Before undertaking instruction some decisions should be made about appropriate materials to use.

Establishing a Reading Level

One of the first decisions involves what level of text is appropriate. Information from the student's school, such as teachers' comments and test results, can be used as a guideline to determine the level text you should use initially. If there is no information, perhaps choosing a text one grade level below the student's actual grade level would be appropriate. You may have the student read a passage orally. As she does, mark any mistakes (or miscues) on a copy of the text. You can calculate if the text is appropriate by working out the percentage of words that she read correctly. Commonly used guidelines suggest that:

- 98–100% correct—this is an independent level, materials she can read without any help.
- 95–97% correct—this is an instructional level, the materials you should use as you scaffold instruction for her.
- Less than 90%—this is a frustration level, and she should not be reading this level text under normal circumstances.

You will notice that there is that gray area of 91–94% correct. This is where she may be able to read this text with a lot of support, provided that she remains motivated to do so.

Of course, comprehension is the goal of reading, so you may also want to ask the student some questions about what he has read. The guidelines here are:

- 90–100% correct—independent level
- 70–80% correct—instructional level
- Less than 50% correct—frustration level

By looking carefully at the oral reading accuracy and comprehension, you can determine a level to begin instruction. The text should be at an instructional level or better for both oral reading accuracy and comprehension. Collecting these data will also provide you with information about the student's strengths and areas of concern. Among the things you might think about:

- What does she do when she comes to an unfamiliar word? Does she know alternative strategies available to her for decoding?
- Does she go back and correct a misread word if it does not make sense?
- Can she retell a story, or summarize information from an expository passage? Can she look for and find answers in a passage if given time?

Chapters 3–8 provide suitable instructional strategies that address the answers to these questions and others. The cases given next are examples of how you might think about students' performance, what that tells you about a student's reading ability, and the options for changing instruction.

Examples of Diagnostic Teaching

In this section we provide short profiles of students and partial lesson plans to show the process of decision making that can occur in different tutoring situations. Variation in the descriptions of components and activities in each lesson reflects the styles of different tutors and the needs of the students.

Jason. Jason is a 2nd-grader who is struggling with print skills. He looks to the picture first whenever he encounters difficulty with reading a word. Jason reluctantly pays attention to the structure of the word as a last resort. He wants to succeed in school and thinks that reading is the most important thing to make this happen.

Jason has a chart and a bookmark outlining strategy (such as look at the first letter) to use when he comes to an unfamiliar word that he cannot

Figure 2.3. Partial Lesson Plan for Jason

Lesson Component	Strategies and Activities	Outcomes and Formative Assessment
Reading Easy/ Familiar Text	**Rereading:** *What Am I?*, Cutting & Cutting, 1988 **Level:** G **Running Record:** pp. 2–16 **Accuracy:** 96%	Better accuracy—good attention to print. Have him use this again as a familiar book for practice.
Guided reading for Comprehension	**Text:** *Forests*, Parsons, 2005, pp. 1–15 **Level:** H-I **Focus:** Picture captions and labels as aids to comprehension **Preview text:** Read labels and captions; Read orally. **Comprehension Focus:** Identify details that support the main ideas on each page.	He could predict some of the content of the text from reading the labels and captions. Continue the book with a focus on using captions and labels. Jason is not using his strategy bookmark when reading an unfamiliar word.

decode. Despite five sessions in which Tracy, the tutor, has coached him to use strategies other than just looking at the illustrations, he still does so before attending to graphic information (see Figure 2.3). Tracy considers some options. She could:

1. Use text with no pictures.
2. Lower the text level so he can practice where there are fewer unfamiliar words.
3. Choose only one strategy for him to use—spell the word—for all unfamiliar words.
4. Persevere with her current instruction.

Any of the first three options may be appropriate. It seems unlikely that he will change his behaviors if the current instruction is continued. Using a text with no pictures could work but is somewhat punitive, and he may become less motivated to participate in his lessons. Lowering the text level could be effective, but a habitual strategy is often applied across all kinds of text. Lowering the level could also mean that he does not come across unfamiliar words so may not learn to use multiple strategies to decode. Therefore, Tracy should simplify the instruction: Rather than allow him to use multiple strategies, insist on one, and once it is learned add another, and so on.

Courtney. Courtney is a 1st-grade student who is just beginning to struggle with reading. Her teacher has noticed that her only strategy on coming to an unfamiliar word is to use the first letter. When she uses the first letter to decode, she often substitutes a word with the same beginning that does not make sense in the sentence, but she does not go back and correct herself.

The tutor, Mark, has been drawing Courtney's attention to the middle and end of words to help her use more than the first letter in reading unfamiliar words. Courtney has had some success with her word sorts, and has reached automaticity with short 'a' families. She has become proficient at the short 'i' family sort, but when Mark asks Courtney to write three of the six words (a spell check), she substitutes 'a' for 'i' in three of the words (see Figure 2.4). Mark considers several options:

1. Persevere with the short 'i' family sort.
2. Review the short 'a' family sort with a spell check to make sure Courtney still remembers that pattern.
3. Do a mixed short 'a' and short 'i' family sort.
4. Move on to a short 'o' family sort.

Figure 2.4. Partial Lesson Plan for Courtney

LESSON COMPONENT	STRATEGIES AND ACTIVITIES	OUTCOMES AND FORMATIVE ASSESSMENT
Rereading	**Title:** *Places*, Sloan & Sloan, 1994 **Level:** C **Running Record:** *What Do Pets Need?* Roper, 2003 **Level:** C **Accuracy:** 96%	
Word Study	**Word sort:** short 'i' rhyming families: sit big pin fit dig fin hit pig win lit wig chin **Spell check:** hit wig chin fit, dig, pin **Word bank:** *what, need* (from *What Do Pets Need?*)	She seemed to sort these easily, but a check of her spelling showed she substituted 'a' for 'i' in three of the six words. She continues to recognize all the word bank words. She likes this activity and is proud of her accomplishments when the words she has read correctly five times are "retired." Add new words from her reading.

Although all of these options could work, the best option is to continue the short 'i' family sort. Although Courtney seems proficient, the purpose of the spell check is to determine if she has internalized the pattern. She has not. Mark should substitute some of the words in the sort with other short "i" words.

Lily. Lily is a 3rd-grader who struggles to read longer words. When reading connected text, she often misreads shorter words that she can read in isolation. In 2nd grade she thought of herself as a good reader, and she has a fairly good sight vocabulary. However, reading has become difficult for her now that decoding the print is confusing and is interfering with her ability to integrate all her reading strategies.

Lily has been working on affixes and has a chart of the most common affixes and their meanings. However, when reading connected text, she has trouble applying this knowledge. When she stops to refer to her chart, she loses her place and forgets what she has read. She is becoming frustrated with her difficulties with long words (see Figure 2.5). The tutor, Michael considers:

Figure 2.5. Partial Lesson Plan for Lily

LESSON COMPONENT	STRATEGIES AND ACTIVITIES	OUTCOMES AND FORMATIVE ASSESSMENT
Word Recognition	**Word solving strategy:** affixed words (from her reading) *poison/ous* *danger/ous* *harm/ful* Add to affixed word chart	
Guided Reading **Title:** *Junie B. Jones Has a Monster Under Her Bed,* Park, 1997 **Level:** M	**DRTA:** Chapter 2 Orally read pages 12–13 Write prediction Read page 14, and revisit prediction Write new prediction after page 14 Read page 15	She is able to come up with some good predictions, but finds it difficult to articulate the evidence from the text. Continue to model how to use evidence from the text.

1. Partner read orally with Lily to provide her with a stronger scaffold.
2. Move Lily to easier text to allow her to practice her new knowledge.
3. Stop being concerned with specific affixes, and focus instead on syllabication instruction.
4. Do more work with affix families to reinforce her knowledge.

Again, any of these options may be appropriate with Lily, but she is not succeeding in reading text at this level. The danger of moving to easier text is that it may have fewer words with affixes, and Lily may not develop her ability to read such words. She needs more support during her reading, so the tutor decides to partner-read to provide a stronger scaffold.

Joel. Joel is a 4th-grade ELL student reading at the 2nd-grade instructional level. Joel's strengths include automatic recall of sight words, and the ability to identify beginning and ending sounds, along with actively using a strategy for decoding unfamiliar words. Areas of need for Joel (see Figure 2.6) include oral reading fluency, using correct phrasing, and acknowledging punctuation. His comprehension skills need to improve, as should his knowledge of academic vocabulary.

Figure 2.6. Partial Lesson Plan for Joel

Lesson Component	Strategies and Activities	Outcomes and Formative Assessment
Fluency (5 to 10 minutes) **Text:** *"Here I Am!" said Smedley*, Puttock, 2002 **Level:** J	Repeated reading Student charts progress	He continues to improve with his rate and accuracy, but his expression and phrasing are poor.
Partner/Guided Reading (20 minutes) **Expository Content:** Animals **Text:** *Silkworms*, Pigdon, 2004 **Level:** I **Focus:** Preview the text and build background knowledge of silkworms.	Prereading Vocabulary field trip Large poster of silk production Text walk **Vocabulary:** Picto-glossary **New words:** *chrysalis, molting, mulberry*	This topic was his choice, and he already knew quite a lot, so the poster was probably unnecessary. Did well with recognizing the words in the text, but still has issues with expression, especially with an unfamiliar text.

Joel enjoys his repeated readings and likes to see his progress. However, although his rate and accuracy are increasing, his phrasing and expression are still poor. His tutor, Mary Anne, thinks about what to do:

1. Do fewer repeated readings and more echo reading.
2. Focus more during the repeated readings on having Joel evaluate his own expression and phrasing.
3. Tape-record Joel's reading to let him hear how he sounds.
4. Do more partner reading so Joel will hear a model of how to read with expression and appropriate phrasing.

Once again, any of the above may be appropriate, but Joel really likes doing repeated readings, so modifying the procedure by adding a component in which he evaluates his own expression and phrasing may be the first thing to do.

Rita. Rita is a 2nd-grade student reading at a pre-primer level for instructional purposes. Juan, her tutor, wants to develop her word attack skills, to increase her sight words, to develop her oral reading fluency, and to help her become an active reader by interacting with text through questioning.

Despite Juan's hard work and perseverance with questioning strategies (see Figure 2.7), Rita is still not becoming an active reader. Although she

Figure 2.7. Partial Lesson Plan for Rita

LESSON COMPONENT	STRATEGIES AND ACTIVITIES	OUTCOMES AND FORMATIVE ASSESSMENT
Reading a New Book Rita and I will revisit the text and questioning strategy we worked on yesterday. To begin, I will ask Rita the questions we came up with to see if she was able to remember/comprehend the text. Then we will discuss our question words again, and the four categories of QAR, and she will complete the text. **Title:** *Food for Animals*, O'Neil, 2008 **Level:** E	Picture walk Review new vocabulary Continue QAR focusing on question words Add to anchor chart **Words:** *few, only*	Rita can talk about the pictures during the picture walk, and seems to understand them, but when it comes to generating questions, she has a hard time, despite my modeling. I am not sure if I should continue with this strategy.

Lesson Component	Strategies and Activities	Outcomes and Formative Assessment
Extending Literacy Today I will take sentences from the text she read, *Food for Animals,* and write them up on cut-up sentence strips. This will give her practice grouping words into phrases of nonfictional text. She understood this quickly with fictional text; therefore, the nonfiction will be good practice for her.	**Materials needed:** Cut up sentence strips, *Food for Animals*	She made only one mistake in putting the sentence strips together. She likes this activity, and I think her phrasing is improving. I need to take her back to the original text after working with the sentence strips to see if she applies the practice.

does not ask good questions when engaging in the QAR activity, she is able to answer Juan's questions to her. The tutor considers what he should do:

1. Persevere, as there has been some progress.
2. Read her more complex text to practice asking questions.
3. Write more LEA's, and engage in questioning strategies with them.
4. Spend less time focusing on comprehension and more time on word attack skills.

This is a situation in which the instruction is not working, so either the text or the instruction should be changed. A level E text may be too simple to generate good questions, so the tutor should read aloud some more complex text that allows practice in good question asking, and allows Rita to think more deeply about the text.

Barry. Barry is a 3rd-grade student who has trouble understanding extended pieces of text. When asked questions about the content of a sentence or a short passage, he is able to respond appropriately. His print skills are appropriate for his grade level, and his general vocabulary knowledge is adequate. However, when Barry is confronted with an extended passage or book chapter, he is unable to make sense of what he is reading (see Figure 2.8).

Barry is enjoying reading *Fly Guy* books. The text on each page is short and funny. He does not have to understand extended text. He is able to use text features to read expository text when reminded to do so. He struggles with setting a purpose for reading. The tutor, Terri, considers her options:

1. Persevere—he is learning if not very quickly.
2. Engage him with extended passages of fiction using DRTA or some other more global comprehension strategy.

Figure 2.8. Partial Lesson Plan for Barry

Lesson Component	Strategies and Activities	Outcomes and Formative Assessment
Guided Reading: Headings, labeling, captions, photographs **Title:** *Shipwrecks*, Ling, 2001 **Level:** H	Barry will finish reading *Scuba Diving*. This seems to be a great instructional level for him for nonfiction as he needs to use his reading strategies, but still is able to work on his fluency and expression as he reads. Again, I will conduct a picture walk and vocabulary introduction.	I drew Barry's attention to the headings and captions, and had him read them orally to me. He still has difficulty turning them into questions to set a purpose for reading, and then reading for that purpose. I don't think he will apply this strategy independently.
Fluency Text: *Hi! Fly Guy*, Tedd Arnold, 2005 **Level:** I	We will also start Barry's third *Fly Guy* book. I will encourage him to change his voice at quotation marks for different characters to improve his fluency and expression.	He loves these books, and he is getting better with his reading rate and expression. I only asked him to reread two pages today with better expression. Continue with the *Fly Guy* books. He chose to do this activity first in the session today, so he is motivated to improve.

3. Teach him how to use the internet to search for information on a topic—he will need to have a purpose to search.
4. Have him write his own Fly Guy book.

The fourth option could be fun but may not develop his comprehension of extended text. The third option may depend on his ability to negotiate the Internet, but the technological aspect would be motivational, and the idea of setting a purpose for reading should transfer to traditional text. If the technology is an issue, perseverance with an informational book about a topic he likes or is familiar with may provide scaffolding to help him negotiate longer passages.

Alana. Alana is a 6th-grader reading at the 4th-grade level, partly because of decoding issues, but also because she struggles to comprehend complex text. Her tutor, Keith, is using a mini-research project to increase Alana's motivation and confidence in both reading and writing.

Figure 2.9. Partial Lesson Plan for Alana

LESSON COMPONENT	STRATEGIES AND ACTIVITIES	OUTCOMES AND FORMATIVE ASSESSMENT
Shared Reading/ Writing (20 min) **Text:** *Amazing Flights of the Golden Age*, Hansen, 2003 **Level:** R	Use ABC strategy to preview the text Read pp. 6–7 Take notes in web-form; we *both* hold the pencil	This was probably not the best book for this strategy, because the headings were not embedded in the text in a logical form. She was very interested, but struggled to make good notes despite my modeling. Try a better text or revise the activity.
Independent Reading (10 min) **Text:** *Daredevil Club*, Withers, 2006 **Level:** Q	Continue reading independently Discussion following reading—practice questioning using QtA	This was my first time trying QtA and it showed. Alana tried to follow my lead with the questions, but I don't think she understood why we were doing this. She likes the text. Continue reading this text. Perhaps just discuss the story rather than attempting QtA.

It is the 4th week of tutoring (see Figure 2.9) and Keith is concerned that Alana is still struggling with complex text. He wants to teach her some basic note-taking strategies that she can take into 7th grade, but wonders if this is the best use of the remaining time. He considers his options:

1. Teach the note-taking strategies; they are easily learned and will be beneficial to her.
2. Focus on helping her become an active reader of text through Questions the Author (Beck & McKeown, 2006) and completing the research project.
3. Use the remaining time to explore some of the topics in the 7th-grade social studies curriculum.
4. Teach her about academic language, and how complex sentences can be deconstructed.

All of the options are good ones. With a student Alana's age, she should be involved in her own learning by asking her which of the four options she would like to do.

FINAL REMARKS

These sample interventions are just examples of what successful sessions with students can look like. Students at different levels, and with different reading and writing issues, may have sessions with similar structures but with differing emphases. We have shown how tutors can engage in diagnostic teaching by monitoring the success of their instruction, and considering options for changing texts or strategies where appropriate. You may want to revisit these examples once you have read the rest of the book and understand more about the strategies that the tutors used. We conclude this chapter with a reminder that you should include students in their own learning. They need to take control of their literacy, so as much as possible, they should be participants in what needs to be addressed, and whether instruction is working for them.

Things to Think About

1. How do you feel when you are not consulted about what is happening in a learning situation? What options do you have in these cases? Do you know of good examples of teachers who have engaged students in their own learning?
2. Choose one of the students profiled. Devise a lesson plan for the next session.

3

Print Skills and the Development of Word Knowledge

Zoe, entering 2nd grade, enjoyed many aspects of her 1st-grade literacy experiences: story listening, book selection during visits to the school library, and writing and illustrating her own stories. Despite her enthusiasm for these activities, Zoe was having difficulty learning to read. Her 1st-grade teacher described Zoe as having an inadequate sight vocabulary and being unable to use letter-sound relationships to solve new words. Zoe was leaving 1st grade nearly a year behind in terms of reading achievement.

Zoe's tutor, Jenna, undertook a thorough assessment of Zoe's literacy skills and confirmed that she was reading at an early 1st-grade level. Her ability to use letter-sound relationships to solve words, and the size of her sight vocabulary, the words she could recognize instantly, were inadequate to handle text above the preprimer 1 level. She was able to recognize capital and lowercase letters of the alphabet and could produce the sounds associated with the consonant letters, but not the vowels. Zoe was able to point to words accurately as she was reading connected text at the preprimer 1 level, and did particularly well when Jenna modeled this for her in an echo-reading activity.

Accurate and effortless word identification is essential for successful, enjoyable reading. The purpose of reading—comprehension—depends upon the reader's ability to identify words quickly and without conscious attention. This processing of print is a lower-level cognitive task in contrast to comprehension, which requires higher-level thinking. With exposure, practice, and "overlearning," print processing becomes automatic, with conscious word-solving strategies used as the need arises. A useful analogy is driving a car: The learner, initially aware of every move, eventually drives without thinking about each turn of the wheel or application of the brake. However, when traffic is heavy, or while driving in a blizzard, the driver switches to more purposeful, strategic driving behaviors.

When her print processing becomes automatic, Zoe will be able to instantly identify enough words to manage grade-appropriate material and quickly solve most new words she encounters based upon knowledge of letters, sounds, patterns, and meaning. These positive experiences lead to more reading, thereby providing practice that further secures print skills. Independent reading in text that is manageable provides the best opportunity for practice, because it provides repeated exposure to common words and the opportunity to solve new words successfully.

The student who struggles with word identification and does not experience this success is less likely to choose reading for enjoyment, thereby compounding the problem by limiting exposure to print. Further, these students are often reluctant to choose the books that would provide this relaxed reading experience, instead choosing materials that are too difficult to provide the practice they need.

We believe that connected text reading should make up the bulk of the tutoring time, giving students the opportunity to apply skills in connected text reading for practice and for motivation to continue reading. We cannot teach children every word they will eventually know; they build their sight vocabularies mostly through extensive reading. Furthermore, the repeated exposure to words in connected reading secures words and common spelling patterns into the reader's visual memory, thereby developing the automaticity with print that is needed for comprehension.

Most children develop their word-reading skills without difficulty, through adequate instruction and plenty of exposure to print. While the instructional activities described here are appropriate for all readers, not all will require the same level of intensity or structure in order to achieve results. In Zoe's case, the pressing need to develop a sight vocabulary will require focused instruction toward that end.

This chapter is organized to address the Foundational Skills of the Common Core State Standards (CCSS) for reading and language: categorized print concepts, phonological awareness, phonics and word recognition, and fluency. The Standards are clear in stating that these foundational skills are not "an end in and of themselves" but, rather, essential components of a comprehensive program. The goal of print skill instruction is to read with understanding in authentic, continuous text. The strategies that address each of these categories can be seen in Figure 3.1, although each strategy may address more than one standard.

The matrix is meant to show possible connections. Many activities apply to more than one standard. Each example represents the main focus of that standard.

Figure 3.1. Matrix of Activities Linked to Common Core State Standards

READING STANDARDS: Foundational Skills (K–5)

Print Concepts: Demonstrate understanding of the organization and basic features of print.

Phonological Awareness: Demonstrate understanding of spoken words, syllables, and sounds (phonemes).

Phonics and Word Recognition: Know and apply grade-level phonics and word analysis in decoding words.

Fluency: Reading with sufficient accuracy and fluency to support comprehension.

Focus	Activity	Example Standards
Phonemic awareness	Stretching and segmenting sounds Sound counting Picture sorting Word counting	**Foundational Skill:** Phonological awareness **Kindergarten:** 2(d). Isolate and pronounce the initial, medium, and final sounds in three-phoneme words. **Grade 1:** 2(c). Isolate and pronounce initial, medial vowel, and final sounds (phonemes) in spoken, single-syllable words; 2(d) Segment spoken, single-syllable words into their complete sequence of individual sounds.
Letter recognition	Letter concentration Letter bingo	**Foundational Skill:** Print concepts **Kindergarten:** 1(d). Recognize and name all uppercase and lowercase letters of the alphabet.
Letter-sound knowledge	Alphabet books (student-created) Word building (Making Words)	**Foundational Skills:** Print concepts; Phonics; Word recognition **Kindergarten:** 1(c) Recognize that spoken words are represented in written language by specific sequences of letters; 3(a) Demonstrate basic knowledge of one-to-one letter-sound correspondences by producing the primary or many of the most frequent sounds for each consonant; 3(b) Associate the long and short sounds with common spellings (graphemes) for the five major vowels; 3(d) Distinguish between similarly spelled words by identifying the sounds of the letters that differ. **Grade 1:** 3(c) Know final-e and common vowel team conventions for representing long vowel sounds.

(continued)

Figure 3.1. Matrix of Activities Linked to Common Core State Standards (continued)

Focus	Activity	Example Standards
Word Identification	Practicing visually similar words Word banks Word walls Connected text reading Writing Word sorting Making words Personal word collections: compounds, contractions, and affixed words	**Foundational Skill:** Word recognition **Kindergarten:** 3(c) Read common high-frequency words by sight. **Grade 1:** 3(b) Decode regularly spelled, one-syllable words; 3(f) Read words with inflectional endings. **Grade 2:** 3(c) Decode regularly spelled two-syllable words with long vowels. 3(d) Decode words with common prefixes and suffixes. 3(e) Identify words with inconsistent but common spelling-sound correspondence. 3(f) Recognize and read grade-appropriate irregularly spelled words.

THE DEVELOPMENT OF PRINT SKILLS

The development of print skills includes word-reading, and understanding and use of the conventions of written language, such as punctuation and capitalization. Preceding this learning is the child's conscious awareness of both the phonological structure of speech and the nature of print.

In English, as in all alphabetic languages, letters stand for speech sounds. These provide graphophonemic cues that allow the reader to use letters and spelling patterns to decode, or pronounce, words. Though English spellings do not have perfect letter/sound correspondence, some reliable patterns are useful for decoding visually unfamiliar words and for instantly recognizing previously learned words.

Theories abound as to the causes and origins of difficulties in acquiring print skills, and these are far too many and too complex to address here. Regardless of the suspected reasons, a teacher's and tutor's task is to begin teaching the child, using time-honored as well as innovative instructional practices. The teacher should begin with what the child can do, and build upon that in a manner that is both systematic and holistic.

The activities presented in this chapter have been used with success in classrooms and reading clinics to teach the foundational understandings, as well as the actual skills needed for efficient and problem-free print processing. Figure 3.2 provides simple definitions for the basic terms used to discuss the development of print skills.

Figure 3.2. Important Terms

TERM	MEANING
Phonological awareness	The ability to hear the sounds in language apart from the meaning of language
Phonemic awareness	An aspect of phonological awareness—the ability to segment and manipulate the sounds of oral language.
Alphabetic principle	Units of sound of in a spoken language represented by written letters.
Alphabet knowledge	The ability to recognize and name the capital and lowercase letters of the alphabet.
Letter-sound knowledge	The ability to recognize and produce the sounds associated with letters.
Phonics	How letters relate to spoken sounds; instruction that teaches how to use this to decode words.
Concept of word	Recognizing the boundaries between words; the significance of the spaces between words and the beginning and ending letters and sounds in words.
Word identification	Pronouncing and recognizing written words.
Sight vocabulary	The set of words that a reader recognizes instantly and without conscious analysis.

Source: Adapted from Harris and Hodges, 1992

Phonological Awareness: Activities for Developing Phonemic Awareness

Activities to foster phonological awareness—the ability to hear the sounds of language apart from meaning—invite children to play with sounds, using rhymes, poems, songs, music, games, stories, and writing to increase their awareness of the sounds of our language. Phonemic awareness, one aspect of phonological awareness, is the understanding that sounds, arranged in certain order, make up spoken words. A child's phonemic awareness can be observed in the ability to isolate the individual sounds in a word: to match, count, and add or delete sounds in a word. Some level of phonemic awareness is needed, for example, to hear and recognize the difference between two words that differ by just one sound, or phoneme, such as *for/floor*.

Most children develop phonemic awareness naturally; language experience usually accounts for its development. These early understandings are further practiced and secured as they learn to read and write. Many of the young students encountered in the intervention setting, however,

Activities to develop phonological awareness in young children are most beneficial as whole-class or small-group activities, in which peer modeling supports the process. Many school-based, early literacy interventionists use these methods with small groups of kindergarten and 1st-grade students whom teachers have observed are not acquiring phonological awareness through the regular classroom activities.

will benefit from specific activities designed to strengthen phonemic awareness through word play and language play.

Closely related to phonemic awareness is "concept of word"—the recognition of distinctions between words in continuous speech and, later, the significance of the spaces between words in printed text. The recognition of beginning and ending sounds in words helps students to develop awareness of these word boundaries and promotes the initial letter as a reliable cue for word identification. One of the most effective methods for developing concept of word is through finger-point reading in beginning-reader texts. Zoe was able to finger-point read successfully, especially with consistent modeling from Jenna. This concept will be elaborated upon in Chapter 4.

The following activities help children hear and manipulate the individual sounds in words. These should be done in short sessions of five minutes or less, and to keep the activity moving along at a good pace. The tone should be playful, with instructional talk kept at a minimum. The child will develop these understandings through heightened experiences with language.

Stretching and segmenting sounds. Model the segmenting, or separating and stretching out, of the sounds in words, and have the students identify the word by blending the sounds together. This is done without looking at the printed word; it is an auditory activity only. To increase interest, use the students' names, or words associated with a unit of study in the classroom, or key words or character names from a picture book read-aloud:

't . . . o . . . .m' (Tom)
'p . . . i . . . .g' (pig)
'st . . . o . . . n(e)' (stone)

This activity is used with one-syllable words. Do not separate the sounds of consonant or vowel digraphs, as these letter combinations results in a new, single sound:

h . . . ou . . . s(e) (house) NOT h . . . o . . . u . . . s(e)
The same idea applies to words with r-controlled vowels:
c . . . ar (car) NOT c . . . a . . . r

Sound counting. Students must be able to hear all of the sounds, or phonemes, in a word so they can connect these sounds to letters. To practice this, have students use counting chips or a raised finger to represent each sound in a word. As examples: for the word *bat*, the student would display three counting chips, one for each phoneme; for the word *stop*, four counting chips are needed; for the word *wish*, three counting chips (the 'sh' digraph produces one new sound) are needed. Use the prompt, "Put a chip on the table for each sound you hear in the word 'wish'."

Sound matching by sorting pictures. Picture sorting is an appealing and effective way to have students listen to and match initial sounds in words. Begin the activity without mentioning the letter names so the students can listen attentively and focus on the initial sounds in words that are represented by pictures.

Give the students picture cards (without words printed on them) representing two or three initial letter sounds (see Figure 3.3). Begin the activity by placing a picture representing each letter on the table and asking the child to identify the object in each picture. The child must be able to easily name these, as they provide a point of reference for the sound matching.

Have the student place each picture under the example picture with the matching initial sound (boot and lemon in Figure 3.4), and say the name of the picture and the example picture to clearly hear the matching initial sounds. When the pictures are sorted, ask the students to isolate the initial sound that all picture names in a column share. Then ask them to identify the letter associated with that sound, and to place a letter card above each column.

The sequence for instruction should begin with sounds that have both high utility in English and are easiest for students to hear and distinguish

Figure 3.3. Picture Sort Begun

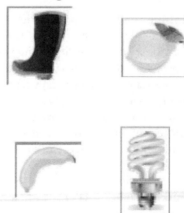

Figure 3.4. Picture Sort Completed

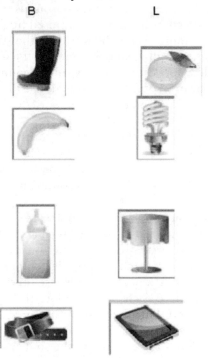

(b, m, c/k, s, t , d, p) and then move on to sounds with less frequency as initial letters and present more difficulty for students (h, w, y,). When students become proficient in sorting between consonants that are easily distinguished, they should be challenged to sort between sounds that are similar, thereby further developing auditory discrimination: b/p, f/v, k/g, s/z, t/d.

Word counting. Beginning readers need practice in recognizing where one word ends and another begins. This allows them to use initial and ending sounds and letters for writing and decoding words. To develop and practice the concept of word at the auditory level, ask the child to count the number of words in a sentence read aloud. Begin with simple sentences and advance to longer sentences. It helps to have students raise a finger for each word as they repeat the sentence. To increase interest and engagement, use sentences that are meaningful to the student or that relate to areas of interest or the curriculum. A couple of examples could be:

Vampire bats eat only blood.
Mila sprained her ankle playing soccer.

Familiar stories, perhaps from a teacher read-aloud, are another source of interesting sentences:

Jack's mother threw the magic beans out the window.

Word-counting eventually should be practiced with print the child can see, during shared reading and writing activities.

Alphabet Knowledge: Activities for Teaching Letter Recognition

Children develop their knowledge of letter names (letter recognition) and the sounds they represent through exposure to print, informal and formal instruction, and early experiences with reading and writing. Children must recognize and name the letters (letter recognition) and understand that these letters represent the sounds of the English language (alphabetic principle).

In order to read words and be able to distinguish among visually similar words, children must have mastered letter recognition; they must actually overlearn the letters of the alphabet (Adams, 1990). This is often the point at which a child's difficulty with print begins. Certain letters of the alphabet, particularly the lowercase letters so critical for word recognition, appear very similar (b/d, c/e n/u, n/h, v/y). This is in contrast to the more distinct capital, or uppercases, letters, which most children learn first. Children's uncertainty in the area of lowercase letter recognition predisposes them to difficulties with word recognition. When an early reader is experiencing difficulty learning words and acquiring a sight vocabulary, assessing accuracy and speed of letter recognition will often reveal this insecurity. Jenna's assessment of Zoe's letter recognition assured her that Zoe was secure in this area.

Games and word-building activities are appealing ways to learn and practice this. In a classroom or small-group setting, children enjoy the friendly competition that these activities offer. In a one-on-one session, the tutor may play the game against the student. It is important that the element of chance be significant enough to overcome the obvious difference in skill level.

Visual displays for reference. Students may be confusing the lowercase letters *b/d*, a common difficulty for early and struggling readers. A visual reference that includes a phonic association can be helpful, as in this illustration of the word *bed*:

b d (Connect letters to resemble a bed)

Letter concentration. This game can be played like a traditional "concentration" game, in which players assemble pairs by remembering the placement of cards already turned over, or by making a lucky guess. This version is played with uppercase and lowercase letter cards arranged in rows. Players turn over two cards in each turn, trying to match pairs of uppercase and lowercase letters. The game works best with two players, which could include the tutor or another student.

Letter bingo. This game works best with a small group. Children can make their own game boards by folding paper into a 16-block grid. Using letter cards selected for the game, the teacher randomly calls the letters ("lowercase e, . . . capital R," etc.), while the students write each letter in whichever space they choose. Most children also enjoy choosing a "free" space. All of the game boards will contain the same letters, but in different positions.

The letter cards are randomly drawn by the teacher or a student who "calls" (but not displays) the letter, and states whether it is an uppercase or lowercase letter. Students mark the correct letter on their game boards, using sticky dots or chips. The student who gets four marked letters across, down, or in a diagonal calls "bingo" and must identify each letter in the row correctly to win the round.

When constructing the game boards, use letters that are distinctly different in their capital and lowercase forms, as these typically cause problems for children. Focus on letter pairs such as *B/b, E/e, H/h* rather than those that differ mostly by size, such as *C/c, K/k, O/o* (see Figure 3.5 for an example).

Figure 3.5. Bingo Game board

B	e	D	M
G	b	r	E
R	d	FREE	g
h	l	H	m

Alphabet Knowledge:
Activities for Teaching Letter-Sound Relationships

Knowledge of letter-sound relationships is essential for decoding and spelling in an alphabetic language such as English. Phonics refers to the generalizations about the relationships between letters and speech sounds, and also refers to teaching methods that use these generalizations. Students who are learning about letter-sound relationships benefit from activities that highlight the most reliable of these and that teach them in the context of real words whenever possible. Through extensive exposure to words, beginning readers will begin to see and use common spelling patterns as a more efficient route to word-solving than letter-by-letter recoding ("sounding out").

Alphabet books. Student-created alphabet books represent a time-honored method for providing children with an ongoing letter-sound activity. Such a project also provides rich opportunities for vocabulary development. Give each student a blank book with enough pages to accommodate the letters of the alphabet, which should be written clearly in both capital and lowercase letters by the tutor. Using pictures they find or that are provided for them, students tape or paste and then label (with assistance in writing the words) these on the appropriate page (see Figure 3.6).

Figure 3.6. Alphabet Book Double Page

Writing using developmental spelling. In "writing for sound," the student's phonemic awareness, letter-sound knowledge, and concept of word converge. Having students write words using spelling that is based on the sounds they hear develops these understandings and skills. To begin, it may be helpful to provide sentence stems using familiar high-frequency words such as the following:

I can _____.
I like _____.
I see _____.
I went _____.

Have the students write words to complete the sentences, stretching out and listening to the sounds and writing letters to represent those sounds. Encourage the students to add sentences to the stems and begin composing on their own. Students' writing can be analyzed to gather diagnostic information about phonemic awareness, letter recognition, handwriting, and the concept of word. Zoe's lesson plan includes daily sentence writing that will provide opportunities for instruction and practice in these areas.

If the child's writing will be used as text for reading, it should be retyped in a child-friendly font with conventional spelling. The value of developmental spelling is in the process the child uses to create it. To support children's developing word-reading skills, it is necessary for them to read text with conventional spelling.

Word Identification

We view word recognition and word identification as different processes. Word recognition involves reading or locating a word when given some kind of prompt. Word identification refers to the more difficult task of reading the actual word. Consider the following examples:

Word recognition task: "Who can find the word 'said' in this sentence?"

Word identification task: Ask, pointing to the word 'said', "What word is this?"

In the word recognition task, students are told the word and they find or select it. In the word identification task, they actually read it. Often, students are able to recognize words because of the support of the prompt or the ease of differentiating the target word among other choices. This does not necessarily mean that a student can read, or identify, this same word in isolation or in text. Successful text reading depends upon word identification rather than just word recognition, and our instruction and assessments must reflect this.

It may be helpful to rethink certain terms to help us think about what students, especially those who are struggling, need in order to read words accurately and easily. For many teachers and tutors, the term "sight word" refers to words that appear so frequently in text that readers must be able to read them easily and without analysis, or "on sight." What many refer to as "sight words" are those they expect students to learn using whole word methodology, sometimes because of irregular spelling. The goal of having students read these words as whole units prompts teachers and tutors to present them in this way only, with little attention to orthography. We make the case here for a modification in the use of this term and the instruction that often accompanies it.

The term "sight word" here will be used for any word that the reader knows with automaticity, and this set of words makes up that individual reader's sight vocabulary. For mature readers, the sight vocabulary encompasses thousands of words. For the developing reader, this sight vocabulary must grow exponentially to become proficient in increasingly complex text.

One essential component of a reader's sight vocabulary is the set of high-frequency words—those 260 or so identified by Edward Dolch in 1948 that make up more than 60% of running text. For example, the preceding sentence has 16 high-frequency words out of 28, making up 53% of the words in that sentence: *one, of, a, is, the, of, those, or, so, by, in, that, make, up, more, than, of.* These function words are essential to the syntax of our language but vague in meaning, especially in isolation. We think of these high-frequency words as a small, essential, subset of a reader's total sight vocabulary (see Figure 3.7).

Figure 3.7. Sight Vocabulary Diagram

A key goal of the 1st-grade reading program is to establish these words in memory. Teachers rely on the high-frequency words to set their students on the road to fluent reading. These words usually are introduced a few at a time, providing opportunities for continuous review, practice, and application. The goal is automatic, or "sight", recognition. This is an area where Zoe needed additional instruction and practice to make progress.

Among a group of developing readers, the words in an individual reader's sight vocabulary will vary at any point in time. For one student the word *tyrannosaurus rex* may be a sight word, easily recognized for that child, but that same student may not have the high-frequency words *could, was,* or *they* in his sight vocabulary because he has not been able to learn and remember these, much to his teacher's frustration.

Developing an extensive sight vocabulary is essential and likely will be a significant part of your work with early readers. This was the case with Jenna's work with Zoe. Her sight vocabulary was inadequate to manage text above the early 1st-grade level. Sight vocabulary is developed by teaching specific words (such as high-frequency words), by providing readers with ways to solve new words, and by ensuring that they engage in extensive reading for meaningful practice—repeated exposure to words already learned and opportunities to solve new words quickly and successfully.

In this chapter, then, those small function words that appear most often in text will be called high-frequency words. The term "sight word" here will refer to a word the child knows with automaticity rather than a certain set of words that the child was taught using whole-word methodology.

METHODS FOR TEACHING WORDS

Several methods for teaching words are described next. Which method to use depends on the nature of both the word and the reader's level of print-skill development? Jenna used these methods successfully with Zoe, using her own understanding of both the word task and Zoe to provide the right amount of support.

Using the Whole-Word Method

Teaching "whole words" simply means naming the word as a whole unit, or supplying the word. When a teacher provides a student with a word by simply saying it, or points to a word and tells the student the word, the teacher is using a whole-word method, or teaching the word as a holistic unit. Words that should be taught using this method fall into two categories:

1. Words that the child lacks decoding ability to solve because of her current skill level. As the student's sight vocabulary grows and as she learns more about decoding words, she will be less reliant on the whole-word method. It is not effective to provide intensive phonics instruction on the spot as the child encounters the word in text, although this is tempting for some.
2. Words that are spelled irregularly, such as *eye, sew, very*. Such words should be taught as whole units. These are words that do not comply with the orthographic "rules" of modern English, so no amount of phonics instruction will render them regular in terms of spelling.

Teachers often do not direct students' attention to the orthography of irregular words because these originally were taught using whole-word methodology; it is assumed that when words are taught as whole units because of their irregular spellings (*where, come, want, they, do*), students need not attend to the component letters. This is a mistake. Although the word is not reliable in terms of letter-sound relationships, the reader still must attend to its spelling to be able to recognize it in later encounters and to distinguish it among other words. This is particularly true of high-frequency words, which share a great deal of visual similarity: *could/cold; want/went; who/why; some/same; new/ now; had/hard; than/then/them; there/three.*

Note also that many high-frequency words are regularly spelled, especially in view of the child's growing decoding skills. For example, a word such as *for* seems irregular to a child who knows only the cvc pattern for short vowels in closed syllables, but this word is highly regular once the 'r' controlled sound for 'o' is learned. This is another challenge to the view that all high frequency words should be taught as whole words with no attention to orthography. Those high-frequency words with regular spellings provide rich opportunities for instruction in common spelling patterns because of the natural, repeated opportunities for practice in connected text.

The challenge that accompanies the whole-word method is one of practice. Students need to see the word in multiple contexts and have the opportunity to both recognize it among other similar words and to identify it, or read it, in isolation and in connected text. The following activities provide students with opportunities to learn, practice, and celebrate the words they have learned.

Practicing visually similar words. Creating a set of word card pairs that contain visually similar words, such as *was/saw, if/it, ever/very, for/from, than/then,* is helpful for teaching early readers to identify and distinguish among visually similar words. The word is written on one side of the card, and a simple sentence containing the word (underlined) is written on the back. Students practice first by reading the sentences, then move on to identifying the words in isolation—which is the more difficult task, as there is no context to lend support for the word-reading. When students have difficulty or err in reading the word in isolation, turn the card over and have them read the sentence containing the word. Eventually, students will have to be secure enough with these words to identify them in isolation, without the benefit of the context provided by the sentence.

Word banks. These are personal collections of words the student is learning, written on cards and kept in an envelope or on a ring. You want your students to see the word bank grow, to sense the progress being made in word-learning by observing the deck growing in size and heft. Word banks are useful for drill-and-practice, providing a ready set of cards from which to play games. Here is one way to develop a word bank in the intervention setting:

1. Take the words from the student's reading or writing. Each of you can then select two or three words (five or six words per session are enough). Write the words on cards. (Focus on high-frequency words for the early reader with high-interest nouns added.)
2. Spend about 2–3 minutes per session reviewing the words. If the student reads the word immediately, put it in one pile. If the student hesitates or needs more time, put it in a second pile.
3. Have the student put a checkmark on the back of each card in the first pile. Once a word card has five checkmarks, it is put on the word ring. These can be reviewed periodically.
4. Quickly review the words the student missed or needed extra time to read. Draw attention to the graphic features, or have the student spell the word aloud.
5. Praise the student by noting the number of words learned.

Scott noticed that Arun, a 3rd-grade student, was misspelling high-frequency words that he could read easily. Scott added the irregular high-frequency words (those that could not be encoded due to their spelling) to Arun's personal word wall and encouraged him to consult it by making him accountable for the correct spelling of those words in his writing.

This method was used successfully with Zoe. The word bank portion was her favorite part of the lesson. Her word ring represented her progress in a concrete, tangible way.

Word walls. For early readers, the word wall is a reference for word identification, another context to see the words they are learning. Early readers will look to the word wall for confirmation before pronouncing a word they see in text. Display words in alphabetical order for easy reference (see Figure 3.8).

Figure 3.8. Partial Word Wall, Early First Grade

at	go	jump	run	
and	got	let	said	to
by	has	like	what	
can	have	my	with	
did	he	not		
do	is	put	she	you

Pat Cunningham (2012) has written extensively on the topic of word walls and suggests that we be selective with the space, choosing words based on high utility and usefulness of their orthographic features for solving other, analogous words. You can remove those words that the child (1) has mastered and/or (2) has a reliable spelling pattern for successful decoding or spelling. For students in 2nd grade and above who can read but perhaps not spell irregular high-frequency words such as *they, could,* or *there,* the word wall is a useful reference for the conventional spelling of these tricky words. Figure 3.9 shows a personal word wall for Sam, a 2nd grader working on accurate spelling of visually similar, high-frequency words.

Word walls used in a tutoring session can be small and portable. Plain file folders work well; these can be brought out and displayed as needed.

Figure 3.9. Personal Word Wall, Grades 2–3

SAM'S WORD WALL

could	thought	said
should	through	says
would	though	
	they there	where were
ever even	their	wear we're
every	they're	

Connected text reading. High-frequency words are practiced most effectively through connected text reading at the child's independent level, or in rereading familiar text in which accuracy is high as a result of previous exposure. Because these words make up more than 60% of running text, the simple act of reading with few errors will result in repeated exposures. High-frequency words that are regular in terms of spelling also provide repeated opportunities to practice common letter patterns that have high utility as the child encounters new words such as "ike" in *like* and "ent" in *went.* Again, if the text is not too difficult, readers likely will encounter words they can solve given their current skills and the support of context for cross-checking accuracy.

Writing. Referencing the word wall for spelling common words learned by the whole-word method gives students the opportunity to attend to the orthography, or spelling, of words learned in this manner. It is fair to expect students to spell conventionally words that are on the word wall; this is another way to give them the practice they need with these essential words.

One way to encourage students to use this resource for spelling is to prompt them to use the word wall to correct misspellings in their writing. Students should be challenged to locate and fix their own errors in spelling, capitalization, and punctuation, and to use the word wall as a resource for editing their writing.

Language Experience Approach (LEA). The LEA is a method for creating meaningful text using the child's own language and experiences. Developed in the 1960s for classroom instruction, the LEA involves the teacher scribing the children's language about a shared experience, usually on chart paper. The LEA helps children make the connection between spoken and written language and provides accessible text for early readers. Oral language is used as a support, or scaffold, to written language.

This text then can be used in a variety of ways: for shared reading, for building word banks, as a "stem" for extending writing, and so on. The LEA is especially useful when adapted to tutoring, as the text created will be even more personal and appropriately matched to the child's capabilities. Here is a step-by-step procedure for using the LEA with an individual student:

Day 1
- The tutor and the child agree on the stimulus experience and briefly discuss it.
- The child dictates while the tutor records the story using the child's words. This can be done on chart paper, regular-size paper, or a computer screen as the student watches.
- The tutor may ask the student to provide initial, middle, or ending sounds; the spelling of known high-frequency words

(the word wall can be referenced); punctuation marks; capital letters, and so on. While the child is asked to participate, the tutor does the scribing, and all spelling and punctuation should be conventional.

- When the story is finished (four to six sentences), the tutor and the child read the story using some level of support-partner, echo, or choral reading. Finger-point reading should be modeled and used.
- A title should be selected and added to the top of the page.
- The student eventually should read the entire story, pointing to each word.

Day 2

- The tutor inputs the story and prints out a copy for the student. The tutor and student read the story together using choral or echo reading.
- The tutor points to random words for the student to identify ("spot checking").

Day 3

- The student reads the story independently.
- Words from the story that have been recognized in spot checking are presented in isolation on word cards.
- Word cards are added to the student's word bank or word ring.
- The story is put in a binder and reread periodically along with other archived stories.

Using the computer screen to scribe the story for an individual child has advantages: It is easy to print copies, choose a primary-type font, and adjust the size as needed. This is important if the tutor's handwriting is not clear and legible—something that can pose problems for students who have difficulties with letter and word recognition. Additional spacing between words and double spacing between lines can make text more readable for the early reader. The following story was dictated by Zoe in Session 2, to be used as reading material and as a source for words for Zoe's work ring.

My Dog
I have a shelter puppy.
His name is Jordy.
Jordy likes to chase balls and play
with paper bags.

Jenna will use Zoe's text to teach her the high-frequency words *have, play,* and *with.* These will be spot-checked in text, perhaps highlighted by Zoe, and eventually put on cards for her word bank.

Learning Words from Context

Students can identify many new words while reading, using just the essential print cues along with the contextual support of the sentence or passage. In reading the following sentence, a student may not be familiar with the word *traditional.*

Navajo Indians continue to grow corn using old, traditional methods.

To identify the word, the student can use *tr* as a print cue and *old* as a meaning cue, and perhaps some background knowledge of the Navajo. If the word is in the reader's listening vocabulary, this may be all that is needed to identify *traditional.* Not all readers have the extensive listening vocabularies needed to access many words in this manner, especially when reading informational text. If the student struggles with such a word in the text reading, it is best to provide it along with a child-friendly definition, and then return to the word (if it is one the student should learn) after reading for further analysis and discussion. In this case, it would be helpful to point out the contextual clue *old* that is positioned before the word.

Learning to Decode Single-Syllable Words

Readers must become overly familiar with the most common spelling patterns in English so they can use these to decode new words successfully. These patterns occur at the syllable level, and are first introduced by learning single-syllable words that follow these patterns: *cvc, cvcc, cvce, cvvc, cv.* Common words such as *can* (cvc), *help* (cvcc), *like* (cvce), *read* (cvvc), and *go* (cv) help to illustrate these patterns and can be used to begin instruction on decoding new words.

Word sorting. Word sorting is an inductive method for learning to decode words using analogy. Word sorting promotes efficient word reading as students transfer this learning to contextual reading. The sequence we suggest begins with learning the "word families" or rhyming short-vowel patterns. It then moves to non-rhyming short-vowel words, then to mixed-vowel patterns including long and r-controlled vowels. Although the feature in each sort is the vowel pattern, blends and consonant digraphs are included in the words.

Jenna's plan for Zoe includes word sorting, beginning with rhyming, short-vowel patterns, or "word families" to introduce and practice short-vowel sounds and to reinforce the use of the initial letter in decoding.

The tutor chooses word cards, or exemplars, that will head each column and provide a model for the student if needed. A sort for rhyming "short a" families might have header words like this:

can   hat   Dad

The student must know these exemplar words to be able to use them to solve other words in the sort as needed. These should be reviewed or taught before starting.

Model the procedure by placing a word card under its exemplar and reading the word, then reading the exemplar to show that the words have the same middle and ending sounds. Then give the student a word card to place, read, and "check" with the exemplar by reading it as well. The child may have to read the exemplar first, and should be directed back to the exemplar as needed.

Continue the activity in this manner. It is best to keep it short, so prepare the cards to make the columns come out even and have no more than four or five words total in each column, and no more than four columns.

can	hat	Dad
man	pat	had
ran	bat	mad

When the sort is complete, have the student read each column and tell why those words go together. Trying to reach the generalization by using examples: "All of these words have the letter 'a,' and the letter 'a' makes the same sound in all of these words." The student then isolates the sound and, finally, labels the sound "short a." Follow the activity with a spell check of five or six words from the sort.

This approach begins with the examples and works toward the generalization. It is the opposite of most deductive methods for teaching phonics,

Liz noticed that Connor, a 1st-grade student, was having difficulty spelling and reading the non-rhyming short vowel sort words once they were presented randomly, without the support of the columns. This told Liz that Connor was not yet secure with short-vowel sounds and would need more practice sorting and writing these words. She also located short-vowel words from his reading material to include on his word ring to provide additional exposure and practice.

in which the generalization comes first, followed by examples. The inductive method used for word sorting allows children to use what they know already, the exemplar, to solve the new word, thereby fostering the use of analogy for decoding.

The sequence for word sorting that we use with students in grades 1 and 2 is as follows:

1. Short-vowel rhyming families
2. Mixed short vowels, non-rhyming (use underlined word as exemplar)
3. Vowel patterns, including short-, long-, and r-controlled vowels

Making Words. This is a word-building activity in which students are given a set of letter tiles or cards to build a variety of smaller words, eventually building the "mystery word" that uses all of the letters provided (Cunningham et al., 2001). This activity provides instruction and practice in phonemic awareness, letter-sound relationships, concept of word, and later, word structure.

For example, students are given the following letter tiles: *s, k, t, r, a, e* (mystery word: skater), and follow your prompts to build words in a sequential manner, beginning with simple words and progressing to more complex words. Observing students in this activity provides rich diagnostic information about their abilities to hear, identify, and sequence the sounds in words.

1. Use two letters to make the word *at*.
2. Now add a letter to make the word *sat*.
3. Now change one letter to make the word *rat*.
4. Now add one letter to make the word *rats*.

Select the words and sequences based upon what your students need to practice or learn. For example, if students are working on r-controlled vowels, the words *tar* and *star* could be added to the above lesson. If students are working on long-vowel patterns, the words *rake, take, stake*, and *skate* can be used. Irregularly spelled words are not appropriate for this activity with 1st-grade students, or with 2nd-graders who are still struggling with vowel patterns. For example, the word *stake* could be used in the above sequence, but not *steak*, because it has an irregular spelling.

Encourage students to try to form the mystery word, which uses all of the letters, but expect to give support in doing this. It adds interest to use a mystery word from a thematic word wall. A tutor can use a prompt such as, "It's a word we use when we talk about our gerbils, and it's on our Gerbil Word Wall" (rodent).

Making Words continues to be useful as students further develop their print skills. A lesson for a student working on short-vowel and long-vowel patterns could proceed as follows:

Distribute letter cards *e, d, i, p, r, s* (the secret word that uses all the letters is *spider*)

> Erica found the Making Words activity to be especially helpful with her primary grade students who were having difficulty with sequencing letters in words. For example, to make the word *send*, these students might select the correct letters but arrange them incorrectly, without stretching out and listening to the sequence of sounds. This activity provided a rigorous phonological workout that helped her students with both decoding and spelling.

- Ask the student to use the letter cards to make the word *sip*
- Change one letter to make the word *dip*
- Add a letter to make the word *drip*
- Take away a letter to make the word *rip*
- Add a letter to make the word *ripe*
- Take away "r" and then make the word *pie*
- Add two letters to make the word *pride*
- Change the beginning to make the word *side*

Although we have seen meaning clues used as prompts ("make a word that means to drink something slowly"), we believe that struggling readers need to be provided the target word so they can focus on choosing and sequencing the letters. However, you should take the opportunity to discuss meanings when interesting words are built.

Examples of Making Words lessons can be found in Patricia Cunningham's books *Making Words* (Cunningham, Hall, & Heggie, 2001), *Making Words First Grade* (Cunningham & Hall, 2008), and *Making Big Words* (Cunningham, Hall, & Heggie 2001), and in online resources. We encourage tutors to develop their own lessons using words and sequences specific to their students' needs and interests.

Teaching Multisyllabic Words

New or struggling readers will have to learn to break compound words, contractions, affixed words (words with prefixes and suffixes), and eventually other multisyllabic words into manageable parts. The reliable spelling

Figure 3.10. Compound Concentration

some	where
gold	fish
fire	place

patterns learned in the early years are applicable at the syllable level, so the ability to break words into parts for analysis is essential. Further, early readers and struggling readers are often anxious about longer words, and need to see the relationship between these words and the smaller words and word parts they already know.

Compound words. Students can find examples of compound words in their reading material, and collect these words on cards or in a personal word journal. Discussion of the meanings of the component words and the whole word is a good introduction to morphology. Games like Concentration and Go Fish can be made using word cards that, when paired, result in compound words (see Figure 3.10).

> Dennis noticed that his student, Amanda, a fourth grader, was anxious about longer words when she encountered them in text. A morpheme chart such as the one in Figure 3.11 helped Amanda recognize that many of these words could be broken into recognizable parts. Amanda added words from the materials she was reading, and she enjoyed analyzing the affixed words after reading. She used the dictionary and thesaurus to help her with meanings where necessary, making this a vocabulary activity, as well as a word identification activity.

Contractions and affixed words. The text the students are reading can be mined for examples of contractions and affixed words. After they read the text, affixed words can be collected and added to a chart and analyzed based on morphology, as in the example below. Figure 3.11 provides a morpheme chart.

Figure 3.11. A Morpheme Chart

BREAK THE WORD INTO ROOT WORD AND PREFIX	MEANING OF ROOT WORD	MEANING OF PREFIX	WHAT THE WORD MEANS	SYNONYM	EXAMPLE
un/usual	normal	not	not normal	odd	A blizzard in May

SAMPLE LESSON PLANS FOR ZOE

To plan instruction for Zoe, Jenna used an intervention plan that would develop Zoe's print skills. The goal was to make word reading more successful, even effortless: to build a sight vocabulary of words Zoe could recognize instantly and to give her the tools to solve some of the visually unfamiliar words she was encountering in text. (See Jenna's sample lesson plans for Zoe in Figures 3.12 and 3.13.)

Figure 3.12. Lesson Plan for Zoe, Session 5

LESSON COMPONENT	STRATEGIES AND ACTIVITIES	OUTCOMES AND FORMATIVE ASSESSMENT
Rereading **Title:** *I Can Jump,* Joy Cowley, 1986 **Level:** C	A familiar book	She is secure in this text. (third day)
Running Record **Title:** *In My Room,* Ron Bacon, 1996 **Level:** C		96% accuracy; error *the/my* Finger-pointing not as accurate as it should be.
Word Bank Words *into came*	Add to word bank and review previous words	**Word bank total:** 22 words
Word Study Short -i rhyming families: *-it, -in* hit win fit pin sit fin spit chin	Zoe has mastered the 'short a' rhyming families, and I want to see what she can do with "short i." We will partner sort until I have a handle on how proficient she is.	**Spell check:** 1 error: *cin/chin* Review *ch* digraph: Make *ch* word list with pictures, include *ch* words in dictated sentence.
Writing Language Experience Activity: **Topic:** Zoe's July 4th weekend	A new language experience lesson. If Zoe wants to reread her old LEA as a lead in, we will do that.	**LEA:** We saw the fireworks. We watched the parade with my cousins. Zoe chose to reread her previous 2 LEAs. She is proud of these and her ability to read them.
New Book **Title:** *The White, White Snow,* K. Bonnell, 2007 **Level:** C Echo Partner Independent	Picture walk to introduce new vocabulary.	Zoe needed both echo and partner reading before independent reading. Continue Level C for next few lessons if she continues to need this level of support in new text.

(continued)

Figure 3.12. Lesson Plan for Zoe, Session 5 *(continued)*

LESSON COMPONENT	STRATEGIES AND ACTIVITIES	OUTCOMES AND FORMATIVE ASSESSMENT
Read Aloud Title: *Arthur's Pet Business,* Marc Brown, 1990 **Level:** L **Comprehension Activity:** DLTA	Zoe is enjoying these read-alouds, and they provide me with an opportunity to work on comprehension. She is good at predicting in easier books. What can she do with this story?	She is able to predict generally in terms of the story outcome ("He will get a pet") but needs more experience with thinking about story events. Continue with this activity (DLTA).

Figure 3.13. Word Study Portion, Zoe

LESSON COMPONENT	STRATEGIES AND ACTIVITIES	OUTCOMES AND FORMATIVE ASSESSMENT
SESSION 10		
Word Bank come said run can	Spot-check in text and put on cards	She identified all four words in text—34 words on her ring.
Word Study Sort short o rhyming families: *-op, -ot, -ock* cop lot rock stop pot lock hop dot sock shop hot clock **Spell Check:** *rock, dot, stop, sock, lot, shop*	This is day 4 on this sort, watch for automaticity.	This is easy for her; after 'short u' sort, she can begin the mixed-vowel rhyming families.
Word Bank jump he she for did look	Spot-check and put on cards. Can she handle this many words in a session?	She put all of these cards on her ring. She is motivated to get to 100 words—has 54 words!
Word Study Sort mixed vowels, rhyming families: can tip hot pan hip not ran lip pot tan rip lot **Spell Check:** *pan, rip, not, ran, lip, hot*	I may need to partner-sort; this is our first day with a mixed sort.	She sorted well using the exemplars as needed. Spell check was challenging: *pon/pan* *hat/hot* Continue with mixed-vowel rhyming families in three columns; include 'o' and 'u' next week.

INSTRUCTIONAL PRACTICES TO AVOID

"Look at the Picture"

Are the text and illustrations designed to provide this level of support? If not, it may not be helpful to invite the child to move his eyes from the print when trying to solve a word. Further, this is a strategy of diminishing returns once text becomes more complex.

Calling Attention to Configuration of the Word

The student may use configuration with success when she knows only a handful of words, but this strategy is increasingly unreliable as the number of words she learns grows exponentially. The following words have identical configurations and require attention to visual detail to identify correctly: *come, came, cane, cone, core, care.*

Providing Irrelevant Cues

Practices such as writing words using different colored inks or on colored word cards can provide students with cues that are not helpful in transferring the learning to another context. Children for whom print is difficult will go to great lengths to learn words by means other than those we are promoting, and these may not always be successful in the long run. For example, a child may remember that the word *them* is written on a yellow card in his word bank, and remember it that way, rather than by noticing its spelling, thereby distinguishing it from other "th" words. The yellow card serves as an irrelevant cue because it will not be useful in identifying that word in other places. We have known children to memorize the order of the words on their word rings, leading tutors to believe that the children knew these words—until the deck was shuffled and the order changed, under great protest from the child!

Elaborate compensatory strategies are often developed by children who have been avoiding print because they find it difficult to distinguish between letters, hear the sounds that letters represent, and/or remember which sound goes with which letter. We are often mystified by their ability to do something that seems more difficult (memorizing the order of 50 words on a ring) than the actual task being avoided. Focused instruction can help these children overcome their anxieties about print.

Illegible Handwriting

Early and struggling readers are trying to distinguish among letters and words that look similar, and spaces between words that are not distinct enough. An unclosed "a" resembles "u," for example, and "t" can look like "f." If your handwriting is not clear and legible, use word processing and choose a clear, primary-type font in at least 14 point when creating instructional materials such as a word bank, word wall, or chart story for an early reader, and leave double spaces between words and lines of print.

FINAL REMARKS

Eventually, the words in a reader's sight vocabulary will number in the thousands. Fortunately, you don't have to teach every word. By teaching words and teaching about words, we set students on the path to independence, where known words become secure and new word learning continues unfettered, provided that the student has been given the necessary resources and tools for solving new words.

As the students advance to the middle and upper grades, these eventually will include the means for finding the meanings of new words in addition to their pronunciations. This relationship between word identification and vocabulary is important to keep in mind in moving beyond the acquisition of high-frequency words and easily decodable words to more complex word identification. Readers are more likely to solve words that are in their receptive, or listening, vocabularies. The more we build vocabulary, the more we support ease of word identification in more complex texts.

Poor word identification skills are often the underlying cause of fluency issues in the areas of accuracy and rate. Unfortunately, rate scores are often overused as single-data sources for making programmatic and instructional decisions. A low rate score accompanied by a low accuracy score (and these should be separated) should lead to further probing of the student's word-reading in isolation, to see if she can read words without contextual support or without the challenge of integrating all facets of connected text reading. You may find that additional work at the word level, with plenty of practice in text to increase automaticity, is the best way to proceed with instruction. Too often, tedious fluency training is prescribed without determining first if the student's word identification skills are adequate.

Word identification, then, both undergirds and is supported by vocabulary and fluency. This is an example of how the different aspects of reading can be mutually beneficial when instruction recognizes and captures these critical relationships.

Things to Think About

1. How do you determine whether or not an early reader is making adequate progress in developing print skills? What kinds of behaviors would you expect to see? What would cause you to be concerned?
2. Consider the relationship between word identification and the student's conceptual vocabulary, or understanding of word meanings. What are the instructional implications of this relationship?
3. Think of an example in which low fluency scores (cwpm) indicates the need for more instruction at the word level. Think of an example in which low fluency scores do not indicate such a need. How do we analyze and interpret fluency scores to target the actual, precise area of need?

4 Contextual Reading and Fluency

Jonathan was a 3rd-grade student whose comprehension was much better than his print skills. When reading orally, he had few miscues, but when they did occur, he would self-correct. His oral reading was often choppy, lacked expression, and sounded robotic. When he read grade-level text, his oral reading rate was at the 25th percentile. Jonathan exhibited the behaviors of a plodding reader—a student with a slow oral reading rate but good comprehension.

When assessing Jonathan's silent reading, his tutor, Justin, noted that Jonathan's rate increased significantly and his comprehension decreased. Justin concluded that Jonathan was merely skimming when he was reading silently. His main goal for Jonathan would be to increase his oral reading rate and prosody, and to help him transition successfully from oral to silent reading.

This chapter describes methods for guiding and supporting young students as they learn to read for meaning and understanding in connected text. It first focuses on beginning readers who are struggling with contextual reading, then turns to the critical topic of selecting materials for early readers. Finally, the chapter looks at post-primary-grade readers who are not reading fluently. Jonathan's profile represents one type of reader who needs fluency instruction, and there are additional ones as well.

Because we are concerned about students who are experiencing difficulty in reading, the emphasis is on methods that capture the art of diagnostic teaching—instruction that helps students while allowing you to probe for more information about their strengths and needs. This will enable better understanding of the students than initial assessment data will allow.

THE BEGINNING READER

The child's first experiences with connected text should come long before formal reading instruction begins. Children who are fortunate enough to have adults who read to them regularly learn to connect oral language to printed language in a natural manner. These children hear that the text is the same with each reading, that words accompany illustrations, and that story language used in narrative text and academic language used in informational text are somewhat different from the oral language used in everyday conversation. Materials read aloud should expose the child to new concepts that will build background knowledge and rich vocabulary, and will introduce the patterns of written language.

With the proper amount of preparation and support, a beginning reader's first attempts at contextual reading will be successful. The material will be chosen to meet the reader's needs, providing the opportunity to learn more about how print works, to make meaning from words and pictures, and, most important, to be motivated to continue reading. Students who begin to struggle with reading should be rerouted as soon as possible.

We begin by promoting accurate reading with good understanding in text of appropriate complexity for the reader and the level of support available. Then we move the reader forward steadily, and when the sight vocabulary is sufficient to manage late-1st-grade materials, we look for indicators that the student's print skills are becoming automatic. For the reader who has struggled or who begins to struggle at this point, we look for ways to develop fluency, the ease with print that both promotes and is supported by comprehension. Figure 4.1 addresses the links between the instructional activities described in this chapter and the ELA Common Core State Standards (CCSS).

Figure 4.1. Matrix of Activities Linked to CCSS Reading Foundational Skills

Fluency

4. Read with sufficient accuracy and fluency to support comprehension.

Anchor Standards: Reading

Key Ideas and Details

1. Read closely to determine what the text says explicitly and to make logical inferences from it;

Range of Reading and Level of Text Complexity

10. Read and comprehend complex literary and informational texts independently and proficiently.

Focus	Activity	Example Standards
Oral reading	Levels of support for beginning reader: echo, choral, shared, partner reading	K (FS 4) Read emergent level texts with purpose and understanding Grade 2 (FS 4a) Read grade-level texts with purpose and understanding.

(continued)

Figure 4.1. Matrix of Activities Linked to CCSS Reading Foundational Skills *(continued)*

	Prompting and error correction in oral reading	Grades 1–5 (FS 4c) Use context to confirm or self-correct word recognition and understanding; rereading as necessary.
Silent reading (transition to)	Stopping points for comprehension	Grade 1 (2, Info.) Identify the main topic and retell key details of a text. Grade 2 (1, Lit.) Ask and answer questions such as who, what, where, when, why, and how to demonstrate understanding of key details in a text.
Materials for early readers	Selecting appropriate materials for instruction	Grade 1 (10, Lit.) With prompting and support, read prose and poetry of appropriate complexity. Grade 3 (10, Info.) By the end of the year, read and comprehend informational texts at the high end of grade 2–3 complexity band independently and proficiently.
Fluency	Timed Repeated Readings Readers Theatre Developing prosody, phrasing Improving accuracy	Grades 1–5 (FS 4b) Read grade-level prose and poetry orally with accuracy, appropriate rate, and expression on successive readings.

This matrix is meant to show possible connections. It should be noted that many activities apply to more than one standard. Each example represents the main focus of that standard.

> Violet, a beginning reader, resisted finger-point reading until her tutor provided her with a choice of finger-pointing aids including rubber "witch" fingers, golf tees, birthday candles, and colorful pencils. Finger-point reading ensured that Violet was looking at each word as she pronounced it, thereby helping her retain the word in her memory. After Violet saw that the strategy helped her read accurately, she didn't need as much help implementing it.

Levels of Support for Beginning Text Reading

The series of steps described next is ideal for the early reader or the primary-grade reader who is struggling, because it moves from heavy tutor support to independent reading in a flexible, responsive manner. Not all of these steps are needed for every text: the goal is to provide the least amount of support necessary and for the child to do as much of the reading as possible. For students below primer level (mid-1st grade), finger-point reading is modeled by the tutor and practiced by the child to maintain accuracy, and to build the sight vocabulary by ensuring that the reader is looking at the words as they are pronounced.

1. **"Picture walk" or text preview.** The tutor previews the text with the student, "outing" new or unique words. The illustrations serve as a guide; the text itself is not read to the child. The purpose is to place the new words into the student's listening vocabulary or memory just prior to reading, supporting the student's word identification efforts once the word is encountered in text. Marie Clay's (1991) method for introducing a new book describes this procedure and explains how to use the story language as a scaffold for the initial reading.

2. **Shared reading.** The tutor reads the text aloud, inviting the student to read at certain points-to fill in a word or a repeated phrase, for example.

3. **Choral reading.** The tutor and the student read the text aloud, together. You should lead but allow the student's voice to rise or fall as the student's needs indicate.

4. **Echo reading.** The tutor reads a page, and the student reads the same page aloud.

5. **Partner reading.** The tutor and the student take turns reading, usually page-by-page in text for early readers.

6. **Independent reading.** The student reads the text unassisted, maintaining acceptable accuracy.

These steps are intended to prepare the reader for independent reading of the text. The tutor should move flexibly among these methods, providing only the amount of support needed to keep the student in the Zone of Proximal Development. If, for example, partner reading is proceeding smoothly, discontinue your part and let the student finish. If the student begins to struggle, increase the support to choral reading. The goal is to have the student read the text aloud with minimal support.

Faith is a beginning reader in first grade. She is in a guided reading group of students who are reading at Level E (Fountas & Pinnell, 2006). In Figure 4.2 you can see the text-reading portion of a lesson plan, in which Heather, Faith's teacher, has planned the levels of support she intends to provide to Faith and her small group. Notice that it is assumed that students will read the text more than once in the lesson, using a combination of supportive methods.

Figure 4.2. Part of Lesson Plan for Faith and Her Guided Reading Group

LESSON COMPONENT	STRATEGIES AND ACTIVITIES	OUTCOMES AND FORMATIVE ASSESSMENT
New Book: *The Hermit Crab,* Beverly Randall, 1996 **Level:** F	**Introduction:** Preview with picture walk Echo reading **Partner/Independent:** Begin with partner, finish with independent reading.	They could have skipped the echo reading here; two readings with partners would provide some challenge. Try this with the next book.

Prompting and Error Correction During Oral Reading

"What should I do when he comes to a word he doesn't know?" This is a frequently-asked question by teachers, tutors, and parents, and there is no simple answer. You want to guide students through text but also foster independent word-solving habits. Further, these incidents of getting "stuck" while reading require that you act spontaneously, with knowledge of the reader and the nature of the problem. You must respond in a way that is effective for the moment and for the child's learning going forward.

Every second that clicks by as the reader stops takes her further from the text, making it more difficult to employ the print and meaning-based cues needed to solve the word and test it in context for meaning. Asking "What makes sense?" is not helpful when the context has been lost. The reader bores further into the print, or abandons it entirely, looking to you or an illustration for assistance. Your prompts must provide students with the guidance they need to learn more about word-solving. The following are some suggestions for prompting and for correcting errors:

1. Allow wait time, giving the student a chance to solve the problematic word, as her processing may take more time.
2. Provide the word to "keep the ball rolling." Base this on your analysis of the word and the student's current capabilities. The student may not have the phonics knowledge needed for the word, it may have an irregular spelling, or it may not be in the student's listening vocabulary. You can return to the word later to discuss its features or meaning.
3. Use prompts that get the reader back on track quickly. This is not the time for a mini-lesson on vowel sounds or spelling

patterns. It helps to write the word on a whiteboard to revisit for analysis later. Here are some possible prompts:

➤ "Try again." The student may recognize that he has made an error and just needs another try. Some students wait for the teacher to suggest this.

➤ "Spell it." This prompts the reader to take a close look at the letters, something she may be avoiding. The student who knows you use this strategy may develop the habit of looking more closely at the word. Notice if the student has difficulty naming the letters. Word identification is difficult when letter identification in not secure.

➤ "Jump over it." Beginning readers might not understand "Read to the end of the sentence" (Is a sentence the same as a line?), and "Skip it" may encourage a passive stance toward word-solving. "Jump over it, and we'll come back to it" suggests a more active approach.

4. Sometimes, the less said, the better. Develop a set of nonverbal prompts, gestures, and signs that you and the reader understand. These are less intrusive than verbal prompts, allowing the reader to "save face."

➤ Point to the word, or lightly tap above it with a pointer. This is useful when the reader has made a significant, uncorrected error to which you would like him to return.

➤ Point to the next word if you want the child to keep going.

➤ Chunk or divide the word with your finger, showing the student the word parts for easier analysis.

Once the word has been solved, have the student reread the sentence to reestablish meaning.

Avoid these prompts that are overused and ineffective:

- "Look at the picture." The picture is not always reliable for word identification. Students who overuse this strategy may be avoiding print cues, holding on to an early strategy that is no longer useful.
- "Yesterday" prompts, such as "Remember when we sorted

Trevor, a 2nd-grader, sought support from the illustrations whenever he came upon any unfamiliar word or when he made an error that disrupted meaning. His tutor helped to redirect him to the print by pointing to the troublesome word and asking him to spell it. Once the word was identified—and it usually was identified using this simple strategy—his tutor asked him to reread the sentence to reestablish meaning.

words last week and we talked about this sound?" This distracts the reader from the cues available in this moment (Cole, 2006).

- Reciting phonics "rules," as in "When two vowels go walking. . . ." Hearing the rule may not help the child; it is better to give a more specific prompt, such as "Look at the vowel team."
- Misdirected cues: Asking a child to "sound out" a word such as "busy"; or to "find the little word" in "busy" will probably not result in success because of irregularity of the vowel in this word; also, "bus" will not get the child to the pronunciation of busy.

An effective prompt is based on your analysis of the word, and matches the student's skill level and conceptual knowledge. This is a challenging aspect of our instruction that we all work to improve. Videotaping your tutoring session will help you evaluate your prompting and error-correction language.

Transitioning to Silent Reading

Silent reading with comprehension is the goal of reading. Oral reading plays a more significant role in the instructional setting, particularly for early readers who are experiencing difficulty. Teachers need to hear these students in order to provide the necessary instruction and support in texts of increasing complexity. Oral reading provides a window into several aspects of the reading process, including integration of print skills, fluency, and self-monitoring.

For many beginners, reading means oral reading. The relationship between oral and written language is more apparent to them when they read aloud; and the sensory richness of oral reading—seeing and hearing—may be necessary for them to both read the words and understand the text. Some young readers, and readers of all ages, experience difficulty with comprehension when they transition to silent reading. This is the opposite of what is seen with capable readers, who comprehend more fully when reading silently.

> Lauren's tutor, Rashid, noticed a sharp increase in rate when Lauren, a 3rd-grader, read silently. Further, Lauren had to look back in the text repeatedly so she could talk about what she had read. Suspecting that Lauren was skimming rather than reading closely, Rashid discussed silent reading strategies with Lauren and practiced these in short texts before advancing to longer passages.

For most students, the transition to silent reading will occur naturally in the second half of 1st grade, or when they reach that level of text. Teachers support this development by providing opportunities for students to demonstrate that they are reading silently for comprehension, and by planning instruction around effective silent reading behaviors and strategies. Students for whom there are concerns may avoid silent reading and continue to read aloud, or they may welcome silent reading as an opportunity for subterfuge: skimming the text lightly, finally being the first one "done." This is revealed in assessment data when a reader's rates double or triple from oral reading to silent reading while the comprehension scores plummet.

Frequent stopping points to monitor comprehension show the reader the importance of reading for meaning and understanding. One method involves marking a stopping point with a post-it note or sticky dot before the reading begins, and giving students a prompt or question (written on a whiteboard for their reference) that they will be expected to answer or share at the stopping point. In Figure 4.3, the stopping point is marked by a star. Once the students reach the stopping point, they are asked to write a short response to the question "What is the story problem?"

Figure 4.3. Text for a Short Response

Sam tied Junior's leash to a tree.

"You stay here, Junior, " he said.

Junior wagged his tail.

Sam ran to the climbing wall.

Ken was already near the top.

Soon Sam and Ken looked over the park.

"Look!" shouted Ken. "Isn't that Junior?"

Junior was running through the park.

8

Sam's dog ran away while he was on the climbing wall.

In addition to time spent reading with supportive adults, beginners need to read easy text on their own for practice and enjoyment. This builds their sight vocabularies and develops automaticity in decoding and word identification. Familiar texts that the student has read before are good choices, as are those that are easy enough for the student to manage without help. One responsibility as a tutor is to advocate for the power of daily independent reading for students. It may be necessary to discuss this with the child, the classroom teacher, and the parents to make sure that everyone understands what is meant by "easy" text—one that can be read with nearly perfect accuracy and full comprehension.

SELECTING MATERIALS FOR EARLY READERS

So far, we have emphasized the importance of actual time spent in reading connected text. Inadequate reading time is both a cause and a result of underachievement in reading. Reading material is the means through which two goals can be met:

1. The need to practice developing skills with success
2. The need to motivate the reader to continue to read

Many of us remember books that allowed us to begin reading independently for the first time—a series that we read obsessively, an area of interest pursued through extensive reading. Children often need help in locating materials that will capture their interests in such a powerful way. This level of engagement goes a long way toward supporting readers who are struggling. Motivation positions readers in an active stance, increasing the likelihood that they will do the work necessary to solve new words, to think, and to respond. Heidi Anne Mesmer (2008), who has done thorough work on the topic of materials selection, describes how well-chosen texts can produce a momentum toward success; the wrong materials can contribute to the momentum toward failure that some young readers experience. Matching reader to text requires that you know about the student's current level of reading skill, have a sense of what may appeal to her, can estimate the level of her background knowledge, and are open to adjusting these assumptions as you work.

Nell Duke's (2000) work on genre diversification underscores the importance of providing students with a balance of genres and forms. Her research shows that in primary-grade classrooms, narrative fiction dominates the collection, with informational text and poetry far behind. More recently there has been an increase in informational text written for early readers and designed to appeal to them visually: color photographs, sidebars with "bites" of fascinating facts, labels, and varied fonts. Informational texts are appealing to beginning readers, who feel empowered by learning through their own efforts. Further, the topic and presentation can often disguise the simplicity of the actual text in such materials, allowing us to use them successfully with children who might be discouraged or embarrassed by the level of the narrative text they can read.

Materials to Match Your Instructional Purposes

The material you choose must provide opportunities for instruction, and the appropriate scaffold, or support, for learning.

Picture books that represent quality children's literature. What most of us think of when we hear the term "children's books" are richly illustrated, well-told stories by notable authors. Many of these books were meant to be read aloud to children and are too difficult for early readers and those experiencing difficulty to manage on their own, or even with support. Think about whether the author or publisher intended the target audience to listen to this book read aloud by an adult or if the interest level and the text complexity are closely aligned to the instructional needs of beginning readers. For example, though the beautiful, well-known children's picture book *Swimmy*, by author and artist Leo Lionni (1963), makes for a delightful read-aloud for kindergarten and 1st-grade students, most of these same students would find the text—some of which is printed beneath a watery, blue-green wash depicting the ocean—difficult to read themselves. Contrast this with the larger, clear, and comfortably spaced print of the venerable *Frog and Toad* series by Arnold Lobel (1970).

If the lesson allows time for a tutor read-aloud, the material you select should be material the child cannot read himself at this point, but that meets the goals of expanding his background knowledge, his conceptual vocabulary, and his understanding of story language.

Materials written and designed to support the beginning reader. Trade publishers and school publishers both offer a range of materials specifically designed for the beginning reader. Interpreting the systems used to denote text complexity can be overwhelming. Heidi Anne Mesmer (2008) has done the much-needed work to confer order on the chaos often found in book bins and baskets and on shelves in classrooms, book rooms, and libraries. Mesmer groups these materials into three categories based on the type of support the text offers the beginning reader:

- **Qualitative leveling systems.** These systems use a text gradient, with detailed descriptors for each level, to organize books according to increasing complexity. Leveling systems take into account a variety of text features including language, subject matter, content, unique vocabulary, amount of picture support, predictability, genre, length, format, layout, font, and print size. These systems are often associated with guided reading, in which these text features are significant factors in determining the amount and kind of support offered to the reader in a given text.

The text leveling systems of Reading Recovery (Clay, 1993) and Fountas and Pinnell (2006) provide a more finely graded system for evaluating early-reader text than do traditional grade-level or basal-reader levels, allowing for a more precise reader to text-match. Cunningham et al. (2005), however, caution that these systems do not adequately account for word-level difficulty such as decodability and word frequency.

In the CCSS, the lexile system measures text complexity based on traditional readability factors of word frequency and sentence length.

- **Decodability.** Decodable texts, or phonics readers, are written to support young readers in using letter-sound relationships to identify words. These materials have gone in and out of favor over time, and currently are found in the beginning selection of most 1st-grade basal anthologies. The concern that these materials produce numbingly dull, senseless text is real. Sentences such as "Dan can fan Pam" hardly make for a story that children want to read. Further, for this type of text to be aligned with its stated purpose, the "decodable" words must closely match the student's phonics instruction. For example, words such as *thin* and *car* are decodable only if the child has received instruction in the digraph "th" and the r-controlled vowel "a". Mesmer (2008) suggests that decodable text be purchased in sets that clearly define the elements featured, as well as the sequence for instruction. Although this type of text will be unnatural in terms of the language, there is still variation in quality. It is best used in small doses and for the specific purpose of decoding practice in connected text, with the hope that the skills practiced transfer to other, more appealing texts.
- **Vocabulary control.** Vocabulary-controlled texts limit the rate of introduction of words and the selection of words, with the goal of learning high-frequency words to mastery as soon as possible. As with all materials, and perhaps especially materials with a single focus, quality ranges among strict, vocabulary-controlled materials. One criticism of the prototypical vocabulary-controlled *Dick and Jane* series was that the language sounded unnatural and stilted, making it difficult for children to use the syntactic cueing system to support word recognition. Proponents of these materials

would argue that this is precisely the point: early readers need to learn these words by repeated exposure to them as whole units.

Matching Reader to Text

Readers who are experiencing difficulties depend upon appropriate text for successful contextual reading, yet these students are seldom given materials they can read (Allington, 2001). The amount of tutor support available must be considered, along with assessment data that targets the student's range of reading levels.

Materials for instruction. For purposes of guided reading instruction, when the student will be expected to read with teacher support, materials should be complex enough to provide challenge without causing frustration. For the beginning reader, this balance usually can be achieved with 90–97% accuracy, about 3–10 errors for every 100 words, and with some opportunity for comprehension or vocabulary instruction. This accuracy band is wider than what is acceptable for instructional level in students in higher grades, 94–97%. In the early stages of contextual reading, when there is considerable support with print, the borderline range, 90–93%, is acceptable for instruction. Ongoing assessment using running records, in which accuracy is calculated from oral reading, helps to confirm the appropriateness of a text and provides a guide for the next selection.

Though it is necessary to know the beginner's instructional reading grade level—early first (preprimer 1,2,3), mid-first (primer), or late-first grade—when it comes to converting these to a book-leveling system, work within a band of levels rather than one level at any point in time. These systems have variety within a designated letter or number, and individual differences, such as background knowledge and interest, that can render two level-J books very different in terms of complexity. Several leveling conversion charts are available from developers of text gradients and from school publishers. The Scholastic Bookwizard website provides a variety of leveling systems to evaluate specific titles, and a conversion chart is available as well, at http://teacher.scholastic.com/products/leveledbookrooms/leveling_chart.htm

Materials for independent reading. These materials should provide students with a problem-free reading experience, with few errors and full understanding. Children may enjoy rereading favorites that previously were used for instruction but that now are familiar, or new books that they can read with ease. Early readers and those experiencing difficulty usually benefit from support and monitoring in selecting materials for independent reading.

Guidelines for Material Use and Selection

Carefully selected materials are a valuable teaching "partner." The follow-ing guidelines are helpful to keep in mind when selecting and using mate-rials for early reading instruction.

- Use authentic, high-quality materials. For narrative fiction, use trade books as much as possible. At the mid-1st-grade reading level, the choices in quality trade materials increase.
- Select informational text that is current, attractive, and with features associated with that genre and form, even for beginners: photographs, labels, captions, an index, and a glossary.
- Provide choice as much as possible to give the child a sense of control. Limit the choices to materials that are of appropriate complexity and that match our purposes, but the child should make most selections.
- Become familiar with the materials available for beginning readers in the trade and school markets. Know who produced a text and what the purpose appears to be. Be a knowledgeable consumer, and advocate for quality materials for your students.
- Have students keep reading logs to list the books/materials they have read. Include a place for the child to respond with a rating of some kind. This is highly motivating, and provides a useful artifact for assessment.

BEYOND THE BEGINNING READER: DEVELOPING FLUENT READING

Reading fluency, as defined in *The Literacy Dictionary* (Harris & Hodges, 1995, p. 85) is "freedom from word identification problems that might hinder com-prehension in silent reading or the expression of ideas in oral reading." In broad terms, it's the ease with which a student reads aloud and the ability for him to "hear" the words when read silently. Fluent readers use an appro-priate pace when reading, and they match their reading rate to the purpose of reading. They use punctuation as a guide, pausing at commas, stopping momentarily at periods, and, when reading orally, change their voice pitch at question marks. They read with proper intonation and inflection, bringing excitement to a narrative or clarity to informational text. Fluency combines ac-curacy, automaticity, and oral reading prosody that, taken together, facilitate the reader's construction of meaning. It is demonstrated during oral reading through ease of word recognition, appropriate pacing, phrasing, and intona-tion, which were not observed when Jonathan, the student introduced at the beginning of this chapter, read orally. It is a factor in both oral reading and silent reading that can limit or support comprehension (Kuhn & Stahl, 2004).

Reading fluency is an integral part of the complex reading process. Although fluency pertains to both oral and silent reading, fluency in literacy education is associated more often with oral reading. It is multilayered, dependent upon proficiency in speed, accuracy, and phrasing, and can provide multifaceted information about the reading process including measurement of reading rate, accuracy of words read, and comprehension (Morris, 2008). Accuracy refers to the number of words read correctly, with the goal being between 95% and 97% accuracy during instruction, and 98% to 100% when reading independently. Prosody is the proper expression, intonation, and pauses when reading aloud.

Unlike specific decoding, phonics skills, or reading comprehension and vocabulary strategies, fluency is a reflection of the ability to integrate simultaneously the three reading cues:

1. Semantic—the meaning of the language, prior knowledge/schema
2. Syntactic—pattern of the language, sentence structure
3. Graphophonemic—relationship between sounds and the written symbols of language

Upon becoming fluent readers, students expand their sight vocabularies with automatic recall of high-frequency words, learn word-identification strategies, and learn how to apply background knowledge as they comprehend text.

Oral Reading Fluency and Struggling Readers

Research continues to identify reading fluency as one of the defining characteristics of good readers, and lack of fluency as a common characteristic of poor readers, such as Jonathan. Once struggling readers become accurate decoders, their lack of fluency can emerge as another problem they face on their way to reading proficiency (Hudson, Lane, & Pullen, 2005).

Valencia and Buly (2004) conducted a study of 108 5th-grade students who tested below standard on the state assessment. Additional reading assessments that measured print skill, comprehension, vocabulary, and fluency were administered. The analysis revealed statistically distinct and educationally familiar categories: automatic word callers, struggling word callers, word stumblers, plodding readers, monotone readers, and severely disabled readers. Johns and Berglund (2010) identified characteristics of each reader in alignment with oral fluency. We have looked closely at both studies and, as a result, created Figure 4.4, which describes struggling readers with respect to difficulties in oral reading fluency. Jonathan's profile indicates that he is a plodding reader, with a slow oral reading rate but good comprehension.

Figure 4.4. Categories of Dysfluent Readers

TERM	DISPOSITION	ACCURACY	RATE	PROSODY	COMPREHENSION
Automatic word caller	Sound fluent	Good	Average or better	Good	Poor
Struggling word caller	Reads known words, sight words; substitutes inappropriate words in text with familiar words	Poor Does not correct miscues	Average or better	Word-by-word Poor phrasing expression Ignores punctuation	Weak because of inclusion of words that do not correspond to words read
Word stumbler	Stumbles over words, self-corrects	Good	Slow	Not fluid	Good
Plodding reader	Is slow but steady	Good	Poor Lacks automaticity	Little emotion; slow and steady	Acceptable; reads for meaning
Monotone reader	Lacks expression, phrasing, sounds robatic	Good	Appropriate	Lacks all elements	Varies depending on phrasing
Severely disabled reader	Functioning far below grade level	Poor, limited self-corrections	Slow Limited automaticity and sight words	Phrasing and expression weak Halting	Weak

Source: *Fluency: Differentiated Interventions and Progress Monitoring Assessments* (4th ed.), by J. Johns & R. L. Berglund (Newark, DE: International Reading Association and Dubuque, IA: Kendall Hunt (2011)). Reprinted by permission.

Instructional Strategies

The instructional strategies described next support oral reading and help struggling students who encounter additional reading difficulties. First, we identify fluency instructional strategies, and we conclude by listing quick activities that support automaticity and prosody. Which instructional strategy or method to use depends on the nature of the fluency problem and the disposition of the struggling reader.

Structured timed repeated readings. Timed repeated readings (Samuels, 1979) can be used to improve reading rate, accuracy, prosody, and comprehension, benefiting all categories of the dysfluent readers described in Figure 4.4: automatic word callers, struggling word callers, word stumblers, plodding readers, monotone readers, and severely disabled readers. This method shows readers their progress on the same passage they reread over 2 to 3 days, making it ideal for use in tutoring. Jonathan's tutor, Justin, found this to be a highly motivational strategy that engaged Jonathan, a plodding reader, in repeated readings of text and showed him visible evidence of his progress through charting.

1. Select a passage or story of 50 to 200 words at *an appropriate level of difficulty* for the student. Match the text to the student's high instructional level (this differs from the 1-minute fluency snapshot as is used with instructional level text). Choose text from the beginning of the passage. End text at a natural ending point. Make a copy of the passage for scoring. The student reads from the original text or from a copy of the selected text.
2. For the first reading, the student reads the entire selection orally. The tutor keeps track of the time in seconds and the number of miscues. Following the reading, discuss the miscues with the student.

Record the time in seconds and the number of miscues as in the following example, where the student read a 132-word passage in 124 seconds and had 6 miscues.

1. Convert seconds into rate of words per minute (WPM)
2. Multiply the number of words read in the passage by 60 (because there are 60 seconds in a minute): $132 \times 60 = 7920$
3. Divide by the time it took the student to read the passage: 124 seconds: $7920 \div 124$ seconds $= 63$ WPM
4. Mark the WPM and the 6 miscues separately on a chart so that progress for each can be recorded.

5. Following the first read, encourage the student to practice reading the passage either orally or silently, then have the student reread the selection orally and do a second charting of WPM rate and number of miscues.
6. Continue this procedure until the student achieves a suitable rate. Use your professional judgment or norming data to determine if the rate and accuracy meet your goals for the student.

Olive, a 6th-grade struggling word caller, had oral reading rates that were average or at her grade level, but her self-correction of miscues during oral reading was less than 10%. Jessica, her tutor, commented that she often omitted or substituted inappropriate words, which resulted in weak comprehension. Jessica included repeated readings at Olive's instruction level to increase her accuracy and understanding of the text.

This activity can be done in one session, or the third and subsequent readings can be done in the following session. The student also could read the selection along with a tape-recorded narration (as long as rate of reading on the tape matches student's ability to follow along), and then move to the original procedure when audio support is no longer needed.

Include comprehension data through questioning or retelling, and probe the student to reflect on how the repeated readings impact her comprehension. Ideally, the student will see that more is gained from rereading a passage.

Also, have students evaluate themselves on the four components of oral reading. This can be done after the first reading, or after all of the readings, using some means of recording. A possible evaluation form is shown in Figure 4.5. Justin and Jonathan completed the form together

Figure 4.5. Fluency Self-Assessment

Name _____   Date _____

Text _____   Level _____

I read with:

	OKAY	GOOD	EXCELLENT
Accuracy			
Expression			
Phrasing			
Rate			

following the first reading, with the goal of Jonathan's eventually doing this independently.

Readers Theatre. Readers Theatre is a favorite among tutors and students, and can be used as a group activity in an intervention setting. All readers can benefit from this instructional strategy, but it is especially effective with word callers, word stumblers, monotone readers, and severely disabled readers.

Readers Theatre is a way to promote repeated reading in an authentic setting, providing a safe way to perform and read aloud before a group. Unlike a play in which students memorize lines and "act out" their role via props, costumes, stunts, or actions, Readers Theatre allows students to read their scripts while standing or seated in front of the group. Meaning is conveyed to the audience through the reader's expressive and interpretive voice. The students also might wear hats or masks, create hand or stick puppets, or use simple props. The students practice reading their parts, enabling them to practice until they achieve fluency. Readers Theatre develops confidence through fluent reading, allowing students to enjoy the benefits of repeated practice.

Flora, a 3rd-grade monotone reader, read orally at the appropriate rate but ignored punctuation and phrasing. Her reading lacked expression and did not sound like natural speech. To develop oral reading prosody, Manuel, Flora's tutor, included echo reading and choral reading in the tutoring sessions but found that Readers Theatre, with the opportunity for performance, was a more motivating strategy that engaged Flora's interest.

Here is a simple, effective procedure for tutors to use with Readers Theatre:

1. Select material to be read. This may be a published script, selection from a basal or literature series, or one written by students in the class or school.
2. Adapt the materials as needed. Divide longer narrations into two parts, adding narration as needed.
3. Read aloud the story from which the script is based. Model good oral fluency by being expressive.
4. Discuss how each character might sound, then model it.
5. Distribute the scripts. Have the students read the script silently or with a buddy. If the text is too difficult, read the script to the students as they follow along or echo the tutor. If you like, have the students take the script home for additional practice.

6. Complete a choral reading in which all students read the script aloud together.
7. Assign parts or have students practice the script once more, and listen carefully to determine who will be reading each role. Have the students highlight their individual parts and read and reread their assigned parts. Encourage them to "get to know" their character.
8. Conduct more oral readings. Have the students practice reading their own parts and any applicable unison parts.
9. Have the students perform the entire script for their own group or for other tutoring rooms, or even film their performance.

Developing prosody. To teach appropriate intonation while reading, the student has to be made aware of the importance of using punctuation as a guide. Below are several activities that Justin used with Jonathan that support prosody and are not specific to type of reader. Tutors often begin the tutoring session with one of the following exercises:

1. Recite the alphabet or numbers using random punctuation
   ABC? DE.FGH! I? JKL. MN? OPQ? RS!
2. Recite a sentence using different end punctuation.
   Cows moo. Cows moos? Cows moo!
3. Practice placing stress on different words in a sentence.
   I am sad. I am sad. I am sad.
4. To teach correct phrasing, write common phrases on sentence strips or charts to practice phrasing.
   On the road, out of sight, in the closet, by the river
5. Copy a page from text the student is reading and put slash marks at each natural break. Have the student practice reading with correct phrasing.
   My friend and I / decided to /ride our bikes/ to school today.

Improving accuracy. Omitting and inserting words are among the most common type of miscues made by students in oral reading. Justin found the following strategy to be successful with Jonathan, as shown in Figure 4.6:

1. Tape-record the student reading.
2. Copy the text that was read.
3. Have the student listen to the tape while following the text, highlighting omissions or insertions.

Silent Reading, Fluency, Flexibility, and Purpose

One of the goals of developing oral reading fluency is to promote the development of effective silent reading. The argument is that through the oral reading, students develop the ability to segment text into appropriate fragments (clauses, etc.). This ability then transfers to silent reading. As described earlier in this chapter, most students make the transition from oral reading to silent reading about the end of 1st grade, and many will begin this transition by moving their lips as they first learn to read. We know that the optimum speed for oral reading is about 150 words per minute, and the fluent adult reads silently at between 250 and 300 words per minute (depending on the purpose of the reading).

Even though we think we are saying the words to ourselves as we read silently, the voice actually is not used at all. There is no simple way to demonstrate or model fluent silent reading, but you can help students make this transition by helping them realize that it is appropriate to read different types of texts in different ways—and this includes slowing down and speeding up.

All reading is purposeful. Sometimes, in an attempt to develop oral reading fluency, we focus too much on appropriate rate, accuracy, and expression, at the expense of teaching students that they need to adapt all three (but particularly rate) to achieve their varying purposes for reading.

One way to do this is to use different types of text—expository, narrative, poetry, newspapers, digital text—and have students read these for some purpose that makes sense to them (finding information, Readers' Theatre, to learn a story to retell). For example, you can model for them how reading to find who hit home-runs in a baseball game is different from reading to find what causes volcanoes to erupt. Accurate reading is necessary for both, but the rate at which you read will depend on monitoring whether you are accomplishing the purpose. An effective self-assessment is to determine whether the purpose has been accomplished.

Over the years we have seen changes in the common issues that students bring to our programs, often due to what is happening in schools. When phonics was emphasized, students for whom this was their only reading strategy did not use other cueing systems effectively. When students experienced literacy in whole-language classrooms, they often overrelied on context for word identification and needed more instruction in print skills. Now many students think that the focus of reading is speed, rather than comprehension. This seems to be the result of the common use of curriculum-based measurements, in which students read aloud for 1 minute, as the only way to evaluate student's reading progress.

We know that rate is an important indicator, but some students are getting the wrong message about what should be valued in reading. Furthermore, most of the important widely used state tests do not have an oral fluency component, so we may be instructing for one goal, and measuring for another goal. This emphasizes how important it is to measure various aspects of reading, rather than assuming that one aspect sufficiently reflects all the others. Fluency is one important part of literacy instruction, but it should not be emphasized more than other components of reading simply because it is easy to measure.

SAMPLE LESSON PLANS FOR JONATHAN

Jonathan's instructional program consisted of five main parts: word study, fluency, partner/guided reading, writing, and read-alouds/think-alouds. Even though Justin addressed all components of the reading process, the primary emphasis for each session was on improving his fluency, specifically rate and prosody. Jonathan engaged in repeated reading one or two times a week, using charting to record his progress. The method helped improve Jonathan's rate and prosody, and encouraged him to be a more active reader. The repeated readings also encouraged Jonathan to think about text on a deeper level. Figure 4.6 shows a Lesson Plan for Session 4, and Figures 4.7 and 4.8 show a partial Lesson Plan for Sessions 5 and 6 for Jonathan.

Figure 4.6. Lesson Plan for Jonathan: Session 4

Instructional Level: J/K   **Grade Level:** Third

Lesson Component	Strategies and Activity	Outcomes and Formative Assessment
Fluency (10 mins) **Title:** "My Snake" from *You Read to Me, I'll Read to You,* Mary Ann Hoberman and Michael Emberley, 2009	Use highlighters on punctuation to focus on phrasing and expression. Choral-read echo Read independently **Focus/Goal:** Reading with punctuation for expression and phrasing.	Paid attention to highlighted punctuation in each reading. Phrasing improved Still needs to work on expression.

Lesson Component	Strategies and Activity	Outcomes and Formative Assessment
Word Study (12 mins) *Words Their Way*, Bear, Invernizzi, Templeton, & Johnston. (2007) **Level:** Within Word Stage **Focus:** Sort long 'o' word with the *oa, o__e,* and *ow* pattern in single and multisyllabic words	Closed-sort single and multisyllabic words with *oa, o__e, ow*	Sorted single-syllable words with automaticity and ease. Is improving in his ability to identify the patterns in multisyllabic words. Use visual elements of the word when sorting multisyllabic words.
Guided Reading and Vocabulary: (25 mins) **Title:** *Mars and Venus*, Chrismer **Level:** J **Vocabulary:** *Solar system, crater, planet*	Utilize text features to determine the meaning of focused vocabulary: *solar system, crater, telescope* Venn diagram Compare and contrast similarities and differences between Mars and Venus	Modeled use of photographs and glossary features to understand focused vocabulary. Needs further direction to develop strategies to determine meaning of unfamiliar words. Becoming independent in verbalizing comparisons and contrasts and using the Venn diagram to record them. Strong understanding of when it is appropriate to compare/contrast. Continue to practice and model why we compare/contrast things and how it assists in understanding concept presented.
Writing: Partner writes on topic of his choice.	Share the pen– alternate writing sentences.	He chose to write about space. He really enjoyed this activity, stayed on topic adding simple sentences (5 to 8 words). Use sentence frames to model adding detail and sentence formation.
Read-aloud: *The Minstrel and the Dragon Pup*, Rosemary Sutcliff & Emma Chichester, 2001	During the read-aloud, talk about the illustrations and have a conversation about what we think of the story.	He enjoyed the read-aloud. Was able to follow the conversation but had difficulty continuing the discussion. Need to provide sentence frames to support conversation and response to reading.

Figure 4.7. Part of Session 5 for Jonathan

Fluency	Self-Assessment	
Independent level Repeated reading (for fluency and word study) *You Read to Me, I'll Read to You: Scary Tales,* Mary Ann Hoberman and Michael Emberley, 2007	Read with expression— pointing out highlighted punctuation Reread to find long-vowel words; put unfamiliar words on Word Bank cards.	First-read did not pay attention to punctuation even though pointed out, so decided to have him highlight with highlighter tape. Worked well on second-read with expression.

Jonathan enjoyed going on the long-vowel word hunt. Read majority of the words with ease, had some difficulty with long-u words. Wrote on cards.

Will review tomorrow and add long-u to word study portion of tomorrow's lesson. Echo-read for expression. Jonathan still is having difficulty with expression. Will tape-record so he can hear his reading. |

Figure 4.8. Part of Session 6 for Jonathan

Fluency Repeated reading for fluency/ expression		
Echo Reading: "Weekend at the Zoo" in *The Way to the Zoo: Poems about Animals,* David Johnson, 1987.	Record first reading Tape-record him reading, then listen together. Listen and talk about the recording. Discuss what he did well as a reader. Discussed what he could improve—Second reading completed as an echo reading.	Jonathan was intrigued when he heard his reading. He commented,, "I read most of the words right, but I want to read more smoothly."

I think he finally understands what has to be done.

Completed second reading as echo reading. Was smooth; however, continues to be monotone.

Will repeat tomorrow and record. |

FINAL REMARKS

When a child is struggling with contextual reading, explore possible reasons:

- Weakness in a more discrete skill, such as word identification
- Difficulty integrating the components in a synchronized, integrated manner—identifying words, attending to other print cues such as punctuation, and thinking about meaning all at the same time

Adjustments should be made in the texts offered to ensure success, and then work from there. The goal is always to keep the child reading. Schools would need fewer intervention programs if time spent reading successfully in connected text were increased for at-risk and struggling readers, allowing them to accumulate the same amount of practice as their peers. The tutoring lesson must reflect this commitment to time in connected text, and to the selection of engaging, attractive, high-quality materials in a variety of genres and forms. As a self-extending process, reading improves with every successful engagement—something that should motivate teachers and students alike.

Things to Think About

1. What reading behaviors or data, including reading achievement levels, would suggest to the tutor and to the student that the strategy of finger-point reading is no longer needed for most texts?
2. What are some tangible ways that a tutor can engage in self-assessment and ongoing improvement in the area of providing corrective feedback during oral reading?
3. Do you know any students who have the characteristics of: automatic word callers, struggling word callers, word stumblers, plodding readers, monotone readers, severely disabled readers? Do you find this categorization useful?
4. Fluency assessment is fairly easy to do, but interpreting the results and the implications for practice are more complex. What are some of the issues related to fluency assessment, and how it is used?

5 Vocabulary Development: Knowledge of Word Meanings

Serge was a 5th-grade student whose parents had emigrated from Romania when he was a young boy. He understood Romanian but did not speak it. His oral English was fluent, and he was able express himself well. Serge was reading independently at a 2nd-grade level, and at a 4th-grade level for most instructional purposes. However, he did not enjoy reading and did not see himself as a reader. His strength was his comprehension. His areas of weakness were his print skills, reading fluency, knowledge of specific vocabulary, and writing. Serge stated that one of his personal goals for the tutoring program was to learn more words. His oral vocabulary (words that he knew how to use) was not strong, which is typical of many English Language Learners. His tutor, Liz, decided to work primarily on his print skills, and to use his strength in comprehension to develop his metacognition. In addition, since he wanted to learn more words, she wanted to address his confidence in relation to literacy by celebrating what he knew about words and to develop his word consciousness through games that were motivating.

Many students such as Serge who struggle with reading are at a disadvantage in terms of vocabulary learning. Their more able peers acquire knowledge of many new words through extensive reading, but students such as Serge are more likely to experience reading material in school that is above their reading level and contains more words that they do not know. Not only do they face more unfamiliar words, but the processing demands in this material leave little spare cognitive capacity for word learning. In addition, struggling readers are less effective in deploying the strategies necessary for independent word learning (Blachowicz & Fisher, 2000). As a result, word-learning differences are magnified as the school years progress. This interaction between low levels of vocabulary knowledge and subsequent instructional constraints may explain why vocabulary measured at 2nd grade is predictive of vocabulary levels and reading performance well beyond the primary years (Biemiller, 2001).

Research suggests that in learning individual words, no one instructional method has proved to be better than any other but most interventions have proved to be effective in some settings. That is, some form of explicit instruction, either specific word learning or strategies for word learning, is generally more effective for these readers than incidental word learning from context or wide reading alone (Harmon, 1998; Marmolejo, 1990;). In their meta-analysis of vocabulary instruction, Stahl and Fairbanks (1986) argue for the presentation of multiple sources of information for word learning, as well as for the inclusion of discussion in the learning process to explore and deepen word learning.

The Common Core State Standards (CCSS) provides a framework for which words to teach students: general-academic words that are used in multiple academic contexts, and domain-specific words that are used mainly in a content area. This may be more of a continuum from general to specific than a categorization (Blachowicz, Fisher, Ogle, & Watts-Taffe, 2013). Students may need instruction in all forms of academic vocabulary, but this is necessarily constrained by the materials used and the available words to choose from. What follows is a description of strategies for vocabulary development that we have used and found to be successful in tutoring programs.

This chapter is organized to address themes in the CCSS for vocabulary acquisition. The standards can be categorized broadly as addressing word relationships, nuances of meaning, and determining meaning. The strategies that address each of these categories can be seen in Figure 5.1, although each strategy may address more than one standard.

The matrix is meant to show possible connections. Many activities apply to more than one standard. Each example represents the main focus of that standard. For example, Language Standard 4(a) addresses determining meaning from context across all the grades.

Figure 5.1. Matrix of Activities Linked to Common Core State Standards

Anchor Standards—Language Standards—Vocabulary Acquisition and Use

1. Determine or clarify the meaning of unknown and multiple-meaning words and phrases by using context clues, analyzing meaningful word parts, and consulting . . . reference materials, as appropriate.

2. Demonstrate understanding of . . . word relationships and nuances in word meanings.

3. Acquire and accurately use a range of general academic and domain-specific words and phrases. . . . ; demonstrate independence in gathering vocabulary knowledge. . . .

Anchor Standard— Reading Craft and Structure

1. Interpret words or phrases as they are used in text, including technical, connotative, and figurative meanings . . .

(continued)

Focus	Activity	Example Standards
Word relationships	Word collections Concept sorts Semantic maps Alphabet/antonym charts Word fluency	Grade 1: 5(a) Sort words into categories . . . to gain a sense of the concepts categories represent. Grade 3: 5(b) Identify real-life connections between words and their use . . . Grade 5: 5(c) Use the relationships between words . . . to better understand each of the words.
Nuances	Word wizard Semantic feature analysis Synonym web	Grade 2: 5(b) Distinguish shades of meaning among closely related verbs . . . and adjectives. Grade 4: 6 Acquire and use accurately grade-appropriate general academic and domain-specific words and phrases . . .
Determining meaning	Four-square Morphemes Using context	Grade 2: 4(a) Use sentence-level context as a clue to the meaning of a word or phrase. Grade 3: 4(d) Use glossaries or beginning dictionaries, both print and digital, to determine or clarify the precise meaning of key words and phrases. Grades 4 and 6: 4(b) Use common, grade-appropriate Greek and Latin affixes and roots as clues to the meaning of a word.

LEARNING WORD RELATIONSHIPS

Some research by Beck and McKeown (1983) has shown that students learn words more effectively in word-rich classrooms. The goal is to surround students with words and to make them aware of the importance of words. This also can be done in tutoring situations. In addition, we know that students learn words more effectively when they are taught in semantic categories, so the following activities use this as a basis.

Word Collections During Tutoring

One way of developing interest in words is to start a word collection. This could be around a topic or theme a tutor is studying with a student or, even better, something a student is interested in outside of school. For Serge, Liz suggested collecting soccer-related words, as shown in Figure 5.2.

Figure 5.2. A Word Collection of Soccer Words

off-side	penalty	hat-trick	competition
league	midfield	striker	manager
premier	championship	foul	tendon
metatarsal	contract	transfer fee	waiver

These would not necessarily be words found in the readings but, instead, words that Serge or Liz noticed in conversation, on TV, and so forth. Making collections such as this can demonstrate for students just how many words they know, and not just little words, but interesting words. Word collections can also be a stimulus for other forms of instruction, although care should be taken not to spoil the enjoyment of making a collection by turning it into a "school" activity.

Concept Sorts

Concept sorts (or List-Group-Label), such as in Figure 5.3, ask the student to sort words into categories that have the same characteristics. There is usually no one right answer, although some groupings clearly demonstrate deeper understanding of a topic than others. This activity is useful after reading a text or a series of texts on a specific topic. It also can be used to activate prior knowledge.

Figure 5.3. The Spitting Cobra—Example of a Concept Sort

Directions: Sort the following words into groups, and label the groups. You may use some of the words as labels if you wish, or think of a new word as a label. There is no one right answer, but groups should contain more than one word.

frog	spray	poison	blindness	hood
defend	deadly	channels	hunt	food
neck ribs	fangs	hollow	teeth	grooves

Semantic Map

A semantic map is a graphic representation of concepts in a related field. It can take a variety of forms, but a typical form is shown in Figure 5.4. One use is to present a graphic outline to a student after reading a text and ask the student to place the words and concepts into the appropriate spaces. In the figure, some of the words have been supplied,

Figure 5.4. A Semantic Map for "Steam"

Fit six of the following words in the six places provided.

Turbines   **Coffee**   **100 degrees**   **Sunshine**

Heat   **Mines**   **Medicine**   **Pasteurize**

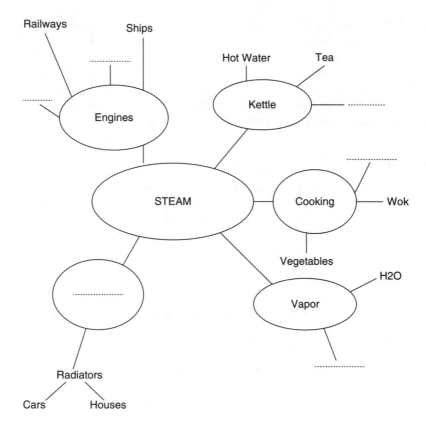

and spaces are left blank for the student to fill in words. Once students become familiar with using this type of organization, they can draw their own map and demonstrate their understanding of the interrelationships. It is important for students to articulate why they have chosen to place words where they do. Research has suggested that struggling readers sometimes do not understand why words are placed in particular relation to others unless the connection is made specific (Blachowicz & Fisher, 2000).

Alphabet/Antonym Table

Playing games that focus on synonyms and antonyms is another fun way to have students manipulate words to develop word consciousness. An alphabet/antonym table is easy to construct (Powell, 1986). It is an alphabetic-generative activity that requires students to use their vocabulary knowledge and, if necessary, a dictionary, thesaurus, or synonym/antonym dictionary. Construct an alphabet/antonym table as follows:

1. Write six words that all begin with the same letter—for example, *whole, white, wicked, winter, wakeful, washed.*
2. Write next to each one the antonym or synonym—for example, *part, black, good, summer, sleepy, dirty.*
3. Now present just the second list to the student, as in Figure 5.5.
4. Ask the student to guess the target words, knowing that they all begin with the letter "w."

Figure 5.5. An Example Alphabet-Antonym Chart

WORD	ANTONYM (W)
part	
black	
good	
summer	
sleepy	
dirty	

Once students have the idea, don't clue them as to the beginning letter. An alphabet/synonym table can be constructed in a similar manner. If students have trouble finding a synonym or an antonym, provide a reference book. A thesaurus may be most effective, and keep in mind that this is often the first time that many students have used one.

Students enjoy these puzzles. Some even learn to construct them for the tutor to do. Serge's tutor, Liz, introduced the alphabet/antonym chart to him, and he enjoyed this activity once he got the hang of it. After the first time Serge used it, Liz wrote

> The alphabet/antonyms table worked out well. I like this activity because it forced him to think of a different antonym for "slow" that wasn't "fast" [because all the answers had to begin with "m"]. I mentioned how this was a way to extend his vocabulary.

After using several alphabet/antonym charts, Liz moved to a synonym chart. She wrote:

> The chart was a bit challenging for Serge. He had been doing only antonyms, so at the beginning he kept trying to write those. Using the thesaurus was a great help. He is beginning to find his way around it more easily.

Serge was proud of his ability to do these charts, and once he had learned to construct them, he took them home to puzzle his brothers and sisters.

Word Fluency

Word Fluency is a technique that encourages students to use categorization to learn vocabulary (Readence & Searfoss, 1980). The task initially seems simple—to name as many words as possible in 1 minute. You will need a watch or a clock with a second-hand and pencil and paper. Give the following directions to the student:

> I want to see how many words you can name in one minute. Any words will do, like *story, book,* or *friend.* When I say "ready" you begin and say the words as rapidly as you can and I will count them. Using sentences or counting numbers is not allowed. You must use separate words. Go as rapidly as you can. (Readence & Searfoss, 1980, p. 43)

Tally the words as the student says them. If students hesitate for 10 seconds or more, suggest looking around the room or thinking about an activity they recently completed. After the students' initial effort, model naming words in categories, which is much easier and faster than choosing random words.

Maria was a 2nd-grade student who had difficulty with print skills and with vocabulary knowledge. Michael, her tutor, wanted to develop her confidence by showing her how many words she knew, so he introduced this technique toward the end of their time together. Maria used categories for his words at the first attempt. Michael wrote in her log:

> *The word fluency was so much fun. Maria left it until last, but she had so much fun with it, I think she will choose it much earlier tomorrow. You know, she named words in categories on the first try.*

Over the next few sessions Michael provided different categories for Maria to use. They had been using informational texts about animals to work on comprehension strategies, so the names of different animals were one set of categories. Another set was generic categories to do with animals—habitat, food, etc. Michael thought that this activity provided a good review of the vocabulary for Maria, and more important, demonstrated to her that she knew "lots of words."

The rules for scoring are:

- No repetitions, no number words, no sentences
- One point for each word
- One point for each category of four words or more.

Students see this as a challenge and enjoy it. They want to try to beat their "score." Once a student is familiar with the activity, provide categories from topics that have been studied recently, such as animals, science, or families. Name only the words that could be in these categories, to reinforce the vocabulary that has been part of earlier lessons.

UNDERSTANDING NUANCES

It can take time to learn the nuances of meaning that are necessary for effective use of a word. Therefore, a student has to see a word repeatedly in different contexts. The following activities can do this successfully.

Word Wizard

Becoming a Word Wizard is a vocabulary instructional strategy that focuses on your choosing words that are essential for students' success in school. The activity proceeds as follows:

1. Select five words from materials that students will use during the week, and write the words on a word wizard chart (see Figure 5.6).
2. On the first day, introduce the five words for the week by pointing to them on the word wizard chart and have the student pronounce each word.
3. During the week, as part of the tutoring session, when encountering the words for the first time, the tutor needs to provide a kid-friendly definition and an example. Ask the student to try to think of another example and to talk about the word while you and the student try to ensure that the student can read it.
4. The next day (after experiencing the word), review the word by saying it, and then asking the student to gives a definition and an example, and telling when the word has been heard, written, or read. Keep a tally on the Word Wizard chart.

Figure 5.6. A Word Wizard Chart

allergic	
permanent	
extraordinary	
adapt	
species	

5. During the week, every time one of the words is encountered (read by you or the student) or used (in writing or conversation), place a checkmark next to the word on the chart.
6. Each week, repeat this procedure, but add new words to the existing chart and tally *all* the words that the students hears, reads, writes, or speaks.

Because the words will appear in different contexts, you and the students might talk about how their knowledge of the words has grown from each exposure. Additional activities are undertaken with the words, mainly requiring the students to use them in a variety of ways.

Semantic Feature Analysis

Another strategy for teaching the meanings of words that are related in meaning is a Semantic Feature Analysis (SFA). You can use SFA to teach the difference between words with similar meanings, or even to teach the meanings of new words. It can be useful when studying a certain topic— for example, geographical features—or when considering the denotations and connotations of words. It is one way to develop word consciousness, discussed below, by drawing students' attention to ways in which words work by having characteristics that distinguish them from other words. The following example of Semantic Feature Analysis uses the word *illusions:*

> Write next to each statement whether you think it is a *hallucination, an apparition, a fantasy, a mirage, a vision,* or none of them. It may be more than one of these.

- Jack was walking in the woods at night when a strange, dark shadow drifted toward him.
- A man dying of thirst in a desert thinks that he sees a lake.
- The priest refused to believe that the angel had appeared to such a sinner.

- When a comet, especially a periodic one, is visible,
- We were amazed at the sudden appearance of this white stranger.
- Susan maintains that she can see the future.
- The dog made no tracks when it ran across the snow.
- In his dreams he saw strange beings that were trying to tell him something.

Engage the students in conversation about possible answers, and model the reasons for choosing one rather than the other. The idea is that each word will have some characteristics in common with the other words, and some unique characteristics. You

> Bogdan was a 3rd-grade student who had grade-level print skills but had difficulty with comprehension. His tutor, Maggie, was using his interest in space as a platform for developing his ability to read and learn from more complex expository text. Together they read several articles and short books about the different planets. She had him construct a Semantic Feature Analysis for the planets that showed some characteristics in common among them (they all orbit the sun, some have moons), and some that were different (gas giants, rings). Bogdan was able to demonstrate his knowledge, and added to the chart when he learned new information about a planet.

then can provide a provisional SFA table, and support students in completing it so each row is dissimilar in some respect, as in Figure 5.7.

Figure 5.7. Semantic Feature Analysis for Illusions: An Example

CATEGORY ILLUSIONS	HAS A PHYSICAL CAUSE	IS USUALLY RELATED TO RELIGION	IS A SPECIFIC THING	IS OBVIOUSLY NOT REAL	ETC.
hallucination	?		X	?	
apparition			X	X	
fantasy					
mirage	X		X		
vision		X	X		

Decide on some characteristics that apply and put them at the head of a column. Then indicate whether this characteristic applies to a word (X) or may apply (?).

Synonym Web

The idea of a synonym web is similar to a semantic map, but it refines the idea of a semantic map, which includes *all* types of related concepts, to an examination of relationships that are *only* synonymic. This type of web is particularly useful with words that have multiple meanings. Although this activity makes clear the synonymic connections, it does not distinguish between the denotations and connotations of words. Students, however, can talk about this as they construct the web. The Figure 5.8 synonym web for *loose* shows how a usage sentence can help to clarify meanings. Students also may use a dictionary to add to the web and develop their understanding of multiple-meaning words.

Figure 5.8. Example Synonym Web for "Loose"

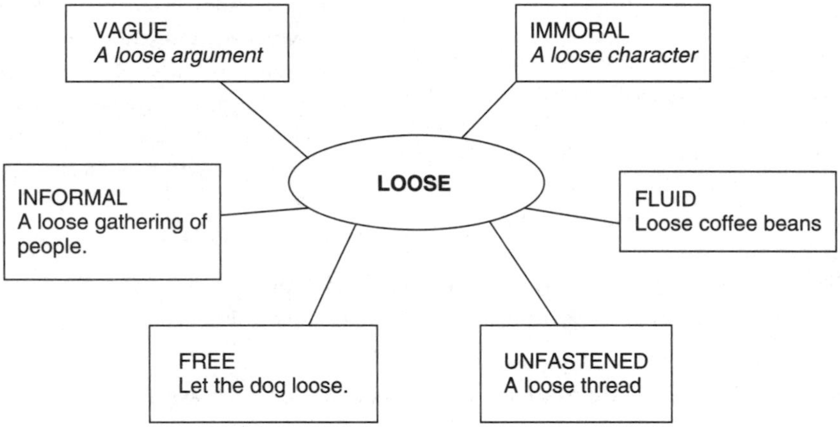

DETERMINING MEANING

You can teach students the meanings of many words, especially if you bear in mind that word learning is a process of knowledge accrual. We learn something about a word, and then some more, and more with each exposure. So it is somewhat misleading to talk about "knowing a word." We know something about a word, but often not all there is to know for every setting. For example, we may know the definition of the term *triangle* and be able to apply it and use it in various settings. But we may not know enough for a full understanding in advanced trigonometry. Therefore, you will have to teach students how to access or determine the meaning of unfamiliar words when they occur. Sometimes reference materials are appropriate, but people usually learn most of our vocabulary from the contexts in which the word may appear.

A "Four-Square" Vocabulary Approach

Some teachers like to use synonyms and antonyms as part of a "four-square" technique (Stahl, 2004). It may take various forms, but two are illustrated here. In Figure 5.9 the target word is in the upper-left box, a synonym in the upper-right box, an antonym in the lower-right box, and an example in the lower-left box. In Figure 5.10 the target word is again in the upper-left box, an example is in the upper-right box, a non-example in the lower-right box, and the meaning (which may be a synonym) in the lower-left box. You may think of some variations (for example, including a picture). Reference materials such as a dictionary and a thesaurus (especially digital references) are helpful in this exercise.

Figure 5.9. Synonym/Antonym "Four-Square"

generous	very giving
Giving to a charity is generous.	mean

Figure 5.10. An Alternative "Four-square"

reiterate	Saying something again so someone can understand.
Repeat, retell	Saying something just once.

Using a four-square approach to remember word meanings provides a structure that can become familiar to students, and also requires them to process the meaning in more than one way as a memory aid. Generating a picture or a diagram as a mnemonic is helpful because it asks the student to think beyond the verbal dimension. Many teachers use this graphic as an effective alternative to looking up a word in a dictionary and writing a sentence.

Teaching Morphology

We have all at one time or another used our knowledge of word parts and Latin or Greek roots to decipher the meaning of an unfamiliar word. Often, we do this by analogy with other words and an effective use of the context in which the word is spoken or written. For example, the meaning of *bicuspid* might be worked out in relation to the *bi-* in *bicycle* or *biplane*, and knowledge of the word *cusp* might be recognized when a dentist is explaining a tooth with two points. Some people have learned the meaning of most of these roots through analogy, but many others were taught the meanings in school. Tutors should teach students the meanings of affixes and root words so inferences about meaning can become transparent and the process of determining meaning through structural analysis will be internalized.

Morphological awareness is the ability to reflect on and manipulate morphemes. The ELA CCSS address the morphemes appropriate for instruction at different grade levels.

Nagy and his colleagues explored the relationships between morphological awareness, orthographic knowledge, vocabulary, reading comprehension, and other variables related to literacy (Nagy, Berninger, Abbott, Vaughan, & Vermeulen, 2003; Nagy, Berninger, & Abbott, 2006). They found that beginning in 4th grade and continuing from there, morphological awareness impacted on reading comprehension in addition to its contribution of vocabulary knowledge. So knowing the meanings of words in a text is important, but the ability to use morphology to access meaning is also helpful in determining meaning. Kieffer and Lesaux (2007) implemented a program of morphology instruction with 4th-grade and 5th-grade students—some ELL (Spanish-speaking) and some native English speakers. They found that students with greater understanding of morphology had higher reading comprehension scores. This was true for both ELL and native English-speaking students.

English spelling is impacted by the semantic or meaning system. Although the "a" in *relative* is pronounced as a schwa (a vowel pronounced as "uh"), students can understand the reason for the spelling when they see the word family *relate, relation, relative*. The system of vowel alternation, and other similar patterns, makes sense only if you understand that it is based in meaning. The teaching of word families that are related in this way often occurs in spelling instruction. In this way, spelling and vocabulary instruction are linked.

Second-language learners can also benefit from structural analysis. We know that loan translation is a common process in second-language learning, and knowledge of common morphemes in both languages can help to make such learning a positive experience. Those who have tried learning another language know that cognates can be both helpful and deceptive. It is helpful that *excellent* in English and *excelente* in Spanish have comparable meanings. However, false cognates can cause problems—such as *excusado,* which means "toilet." Theorists and educators differ on the usefulness of teaching cognates, but learners *will* still engage in loan translation. Consequently, morpheme instruction may play a positive role with second-language learners.

The following is an example of a lesson for teaching particular morphemes—the root *graph* and the prefix *tele*:

1. Ask students to write the word *telephone*. Share with them that the prefix *tele* means "over a distance." Explain that the root *phon* has a meaning about sound (as in *phonics*). Ask them how this helps them to understand the meaning of *telephone*. Now ask them to generate more *tele* words (for example, *telegram, telescope, television, televise, telephoto, telegraph*). Ask them how the meaning over a distance helps them understand the meaning of each word.
2. Ask the students to write the word *telegraph*. Tell them that the root *graph* means "about writing." Ask them how this helps them to understand the meaning of the word. Have them generate words that include *graph* (for example, *paragraph, photograph, monograph, autograph, geography*). Ask them how the meaning about writing helps them to understand the meaning of the words.
3. Ask the students to choose one of the words they generated—for example, *monograph*—and generate more words with the same morpheme (other than *graph* and *tele*).

Extension

Have students use *tele* and *graph* in combination with other roots and affixes to build "crazy words" for which they must write a definition. Have them choose the best word of the ones they make, then illustrate it, and display it.

Carlisle (2000) has suggested decomposition and derivation exercises to teach students how morphology can help to determine a word's meaning. The exercises use analogy to make the relationship between words apparent (see Figures 5.11 and 5.12).

Figure 5.11. Morphology Exercise—Decomposition

Instructions: Look at the word in the first column. Complete the sentence with the root word.

criminal	The young man insisted he did not commit the _____.
tasteless	The hamburger had no _____.
modification	He was not sure how to _____ the bike to make it go faster.
athletic	The _____ was so proud to win the gold medal.
innocence	The jury found the prisoner _____.
reasonable	He told the teacher he had a good _____ for missing class.

Figure 5.12. Morphology Lesson—Derivation

Instructions: Look at the root word on the left and complete the sentence by adding the root word plus a suffix.

evident	The case against the defendant was dismissed for lack of _____.
wonder	They all thought that the fair was _____.
illustrate	The book had won prizes for the colorful _____.
provide	Mom went to the store to buy _____ for the camping trip.
replace	She was not upset, because the broken dish was _____.

Teaching the Use of Context

Contextual word learning is not an easy strategy to master even though most words are learned from context. Several research studies have provided intensive instruction in contextual analysis, but with mixed results (Jenkins, Stein, & Wysocki, 1984). However, some work suggests that a metacognitive focus can be helpful (Kuhn & Stahl, 1998). Evidence seems to be limited for the benefit of teaching certain context frames (for example, *definition, restatement, example, comparison*), because such frames occur relatively infrequently in regular text. The exception consists of textbooks, in which such frames are often used to teach important concepts. Students should be aware of how this works, but in most instances, these concepts will be taught in depth by the teacher—or the textbook has a good glossary. The tutoring situation provides greater opportunity to engage in instruction about how context works to constrain meaning in narrative or other forms of expository text. We like to suggest students "look in the word" for analogies to other words they know, and "around the word" for information from the sentence, paragraph, illustration, and so on. For example, you could use the following passage:

> Mastodons are animals that lived thousands of years ago. We have learned about this *prehistoric* relative of the elephant through *fossil* bones and teeth found all over the world. Some experts believe that mastodons were once as common as buffalo in the western plains of the United States. Mastodons lived at the end of the Ice Age, when *glaciers* were retreating north, leaving many lakes and bogs among hills of crushed rocks, sand, and soil. These swamps and *bogs* were excellent places for mastodons to find the evergreens that they fed on, but they were also death traps. The heavy clay in soft-bottomed pits clung to them and prevented them from climbing the sometimes steep sides. The trapped mastodons became the fossilized bones that have enabled us to learn about them.

You might read this passage, stopping at each of the italicized words and asking,

If I look "in the word," I think that *prehistoric* has something to do with history. If I look "around the word," I can see what clues are there in the sentence and the passage. . . . The previous sentence talks about thousands of years ago. These relatives must have lived then, so "prehistoric" must be something that existed thousands of years ago. Do I need to know any more to understand the passage?

Some of the words (for example, *prehistoric* and *bogs*) can be used to model the concept that enough is known to comprehend the passage, and to show the contextual information that provides clues to the word's meaning. Others (such as *fossils* and *glaciers*) might be used to model the concept that more information may be needed from external sources, such as a dictionary or glossary, to understand the passage.

DEVELOPING WORD CONSCIOUSNESS

Earlier we talked about the importance of word-rich environments. Graves (2006) defined "word consciousness" as "an awareness of and interest in words and their meanings" (p. 7). Nagy (2005) elaborated, stating that word *consciousness* includes "various aspects of words—their meanings, their histories, relationships with other words, word parts, and most importantly, the way writers use words effectively to communicate" (p. 30). Students can develop word consciousness through manipulating words in a variety of ways, both simple and more complex, and many of the activities described here are of this nature. Games with words (or activities that appear game-like) are also effective (Blachowicz & Fisher, 2004). Word play calls on students to reflect metacognitively on words, word parts, and context.

The ability to reflect on, manipulate, combine, and recombine the components of words is a necessary part of vocabulary learning. Phonemic awareness, morphological awareness, and syntactic awareness can all be developed in this way. As students play with words, they develop understanding of word relatedness and domains of meaning through rehearsal and practice. Many students have not had the opportunity to objectify words by manipulating them, and they come to tutoring "afraid" of words. Making word learning fun is an important aspect of what we can do in tutoring.

SAMPLE LESSON PLANS FOR SERGE

Serge entered tutoring as a 5th-grade student reading at a 4th-grade level for instructional purposes. The goals of his tutor, Liz, were to develop his knowledge of vowel/consonant digraphs, to improve his oral reading fluency, to improve his metacognition in relation to comprehension, to develop his self-esteem by working on learning "difficult words," and to develop his writing (particularly expository writing). (See Liz's sample lesson plans for Serge in Figures 5.13 and 5.14.)

Figure 5.13. Lesson Plan for Serge, Session 6

LESSON COMPONENT	STRATEGIES AND ACTIVITIES	OUTCOMES AND FORMATIVE ASSESSMENT
Fluency (10 mins) **Title:** *Long Gray Norris*, Doyle & Walker, 2003 **Level:** M	Repeated reading—graph results **Focus/Goal:** Reading in phrasing and with good rate. Focus on reading with punctuation naturally.	He increased his reading rate from 70 wpm to 95 wpm with better use of phrasing. Still needs to work on expression.
Word study (10 mins) **Focus:** Making words that contain target vowel digraph patterns. *Ow, ou* patterns	**Magic word:** townhouse now how show snow town shown shout house	He did fine with the *ow* pattern; reversed the 'o' and 'u' for *house*. Was able to generate more *ow* words, but could think of only "out" and "mouse" for *ou*. Continue this as a word sort for automaticity.
Guided reading and vocabulary (25 mins) **Title:** *Wildfire Alert!*, Peppas, 2004. **Level:** Q	Teach him to use context to determine the meaning of *canopy, combustion, drought, flammable, insulate* **QAR:** Alternate asking questions that are "right there, think and search, author and me, on my own." Provide evidence for our answers.	He seemed to understand my modeling context use. Needs further direction to develop this ability. He does well in answering all levels of questions but cannot generate the inferential components without help. Continue to practice QAR and model how to form "think and search" questions.
Writing: (10 mins) Summary–GIST **Title:** *Pacal: A Maya King*, MacDonald, 2004. **Level:** P+	This is the first time we have done GIST. I will model summarizing the first paragraph, and we will do the second together. Then we will see if he needs additional support before he does one himself.	He liked this activity and was able to generate a summary. Needs instruction on what is a good summary.

LESSON COMPONENT	STRATEGIES AND ACTIVITIES	OUTCOMES AND FORMATIVE ASSESSMENT
Vocabulary Alphabet/ Antonym Table	Do one, to reinforce his understanding of antonyms, and to develop word consciousness. Help him construct one to take home.	He likes this, and was able to begin with his own words and use a thesaurus to complete it. Continue for motivation and word learning.

Figure 5.14. Partial Lesson Plan for Serge

LESSON COMPONENT	STRATEGIES AND ACTIVITIES	OUTCOMES AND FORMATIVE ASSESSMENT
Session 10		
Guided reading and **vocabulary** (25 mins) **Title:** *Volcano Alert*, Challen, 2004	Review the words *dormant, fissures, pyroclastic, suffocated, tsunami* Have him identify unfamiliar words as we partner read, and use context or resources to determine the meaning.	Serge is beginning to make some good approximations by using context. He identified a meaning of five of seven unfamiliar words he encountered. Continue to practice this without review of important words.
Vocabulary Synonym web	Model how to construct one with the word *harbor*. Have him choose another multi-meaning word he wants to learn, and construct a synonym web.	He likes learning new words, and this helped him with connotations. Include this again to develop word consciousness.
Session 12		
Guided reading and vocabulary (25 mins) **Title:** *Volcano!*, Geiger, 2007	Have him choose one of the chapters to read. Read silently, stopping after each page to do ReQAR. I will choose words which may be unfamiliar on each page, and we will use context or the glossary to determine meanings. I will put these words on our content word wall for review.	He was able to generate good questions after reading each page. At the selected words he managed to identify a meaning for all of them from context, except one for which he used a thesaurus. Give him control of all the processes for the next session.

(continued)

Figure 5.14. Partial Lesson Plan for Serge *(continued)*

LESSON COMPONENT	STRATEGIES AND ACTIVITIES	OUTCOMES AND FORMATIVE ASSESSMENT
Vocabulary Word fluency	He likes this activity: Have him name as many words about volcanoes as he can in one minute.	He managed 17 words and wants to try to beat that tomorrow. Serge seems to like a contest, even against himself.

Things to Think About

1. In your regular reading, keep a journal of some words for which you do not know the meaning. How much do you know about each word—an idea of what it might mean, a possible usage? How did the context in which the word appeared help you to work out a meaning? Use a resource of some kind to find the meaning. What implications does this activity have for your classroom vocabulary instruction?

2. Select a passage you think you could use, and choose words that you think it would be important to teach your students. Ask the students to choose words from the passage that *they* think are important, and that they want to learn. Is there much commonality between the lists? Ask the students if they know the meanings of the words you chose.

3. Examine a list of morphemes (excluding affixes) that are recommended for instruction at your grade level. How many of them did you know the meaning of before you looked at the list? Try to generate at least six words that use each morpheme.

6 Oral Language and Literacy

Alicia was an English Language Learner [ELL] enrolled in a 4th-grade English only classroom. In prekindergarten through 2nd grade, she had been enrolled in a bilingual classroom and transitioned easily from Spanish to English in the middle of 2nd grade. She entered the tutoring program reading at the 2nd-grade instructional level with strength in word recognition, application of spelling patterns, and oral reading rate. In nonacademic settings, Alicia easily communicated with her peers and used a variety of sentence patterns, but at times she made grammatical or pronunciation errors, which rarely interfered with the intent of the conversation. Yet, when discussing content, she made grammatical or pronunciation errors and had difficulty expressing complete thoughts in her first and second languages. At times, this frustrated her and interfered with her ability to discuss content materials.

When assessing Alicia, her tutor, Daniella, noted that Alicia had difficulty self-monitoring for oral reading accuracy and understanding the meaning of comprehension questions in each area of the reading assessment (listening, oral reading, and silent reading), often requiring further teacher prompting, which frequently resulted in a limited response. Daniella concluded that Alicia's lack of familiarity with "question language" and current vocabulary knowledge accounted for some of her difficulty in answering comprehension questions and expressing her ideas. Daniella's main goal for Alicia was to develop her academic language and vocabulary knowledge to support her reading oral communication and comprehension.

Alicia was typical of many ELLs who face challenges as second-language learners when instruction is in English, but at home they speak their native language. It is vital for learners such as Alicia not only to hear school English but also to practice it through discussions and conversations. Therefore, an important component of any tutoring session with ELLs is to engage with them in dialogue, whether about things and events in their personal lives (for example, holidays and celebrations) or about school subject matter. They should have opportunities for conversation but also times for more formal discussion.

This chapter is organized to address themes in the Common Core State Standards (CCSS) for speaking and listening. The standards can be broadly categorized as addressing comprehension and collaboration through structured conversation and presentation and sharing knowledge of ideas through listening and speaking. The strategies that address each of these categories can be seen in Figure 6.1, although each strategy may address more than one standard.

Figure 6.1. Matrix of Activities Linked to Common Core State Standards

Anchor Standards – Language Standards – Speaking and Listening

1. Prepare for and participate effectively in a range of conversations and collaborations with diverse partners, building on others' ideas and expressing their own ideas clearly and persuasively.

2. Integrate and evaluate information presented in diverse media and formats, including visually, quantitatively, and orally.

3. Evaluate a speaker's point of view, reasoning, and use of evidence and rhetoric.

4. Present information, findings, and supporting evidence so listeners can follow the line of reasoning and the organization, development, and style are appropriate to task, purpose, and audience.

5. Make strategic use of digital media and visual displays of data to express information and enhance understanding of presentations.

6. Adapt speech to a variety of contexts and communicative tasks, demonstrating command of formal English when indicated or appropriate.

FOCUS	ACTIVITY	EXAMPLE STANDARDS
Collaborative conversations	Say something; Language frames	Grade 1 SL 1.1 Build on others' talk in conversations by responding to the comments of others.
		Grade 3.1c Ask questions to check understanding of information presented, stay on topic, and link students' comments to the remarks of others.
		Grade 5 SL 5.1c Pose and respond to specific questions by making comments that contribute to the discussion and elaborate on the remarks of others.
		Grade 7 SL 7.1c Pose questions that elicit elaboration and respond to others' questions and comments with relevant observations and ideas that bring back the discussion to topic as needed.

Focus	Activity	Example Standards
Integrate and evaluate information	PRC2	Grade 2 SL 2.2 Build on others' talk in conversations by linking students' comments to the remarks of others.
		Grades 2–3 Ask and answer questions about what a speaker says, to clarify comprehension, gather additional information, or deepen understanding of a topic or issue.
		Grade 4 SL 4.2 Paraphrase portions of a text read aloud.
Evidence to support importance	Thick & thin questions	Grade 2 SL 2.3 Ask and answer questions about what a speaker says, to clarify comprehension, gather additional information, or deepen understanding of a topic or issue.
		Grade 4 SL 4.3 Identify the reasons and evidence that a speaker provides to support specific points.
		Grade 8 SL 8.3 Delineate a speaker's argument and specific claims, evaluating the soundness of the reasoning and relevance and sufficiency of the evidence and identifying when irrelevant evidence is introduced.
Logical presentation of information	PRC2	Grade 2 SL 2.3 Recount with appropriate facts and relevant, descriptive details, speaking audibly in coherent sentences.
		Grade 5 SL 5.4 Report on a text using appropriate facts and relevant, descriptive details to support main ideas or themes; speak clearly at an understandable pace.
Use of visuals to enhance understanding concept presented	Vocabulary visits	Grade 2 SL 2.5 Use visual displays to clarify ideas.
		Grade 5 SL5.5 Use visual displays to enhance the development of main ideas or themes.
Adapt speech to context/task Demonstrate command of English language	Language frames	Grade 1 SL1.6 Produce complete sentences when appropriate to task and situation.
		Grades K–8 SL Adapt speech to a variety of contexts and tasks, using formal English when appropriate to task and situation.

The matrix is meant to show possible connections. Many activities apply to more than one standard. Each example represents the main focus of that standard.

THE IMPORTANCE OF ORAL LANGUAGE

The primary way we communicate is through oral language. It is the gateway for learning, and it facilitates the acquisition of new knowledge. As students' practice and experience oral language, they develop skills in phonology, basic speech patterns and accepted rules of pronunciation; morphology; syntax, how individual words are combined to create sentences; semantics, ways in which language conveys meaning; pragmatics; and the contextually appropriate use of language. There is a natural cumulative progression of oral language development ranging from the simple to the more complex. We need to help students build their language effectively.

Language helps to shape our individual and collective identities. Addressing language issues can be sensitive, and care is needed to celebrate what students can do, rather than to focus on what they cannot do. Further, embedding language development in daily literacy activities extends learning for all students and takes advantage of the powerful influence of purposeful language. The following research supports the relationship of oral language and literacy:

- Thoughts are socially constructed (Vygotsky, 1987)
- Language learning proceeds best when children use language for meaningful purposes (Au, 1998)
- Language learning proceeds best when children are encouraged to take risks, experiment, and make mistakes (Wells, 1986)
- Reading, writing, listening, speaking, and thinking develop in an integrated manner (Au, 1998)
- What constitutes meaningful language use is influenced by an individual's prior experience, culture, motivation, and goals (Delpit, 1995)

These principles of oral language and literacy development seem to hold true both for native English speakers and for students learning English as a second language (Watts-Taffe & Truscott, 2000).

Second-Language Acquisition

Second-language acquisition is the process of learning another language in addition to the native or first language. Second-language acquisition is not unlike first-language acquisition, as it involves the learning of discourse and communicative functions of language, involves cognition, and is often characterized by stages of learning and development. Cummins (1979) theorizes that there is a common underlying proficiency (CUP) between two languages. The skills, ideas, and concepts that students learn in their first language will be transferred to the second language. The implication of CUP is the importance of recognizing that students, even at the very beginning level of second-language acquisition, know something about their new language (Xu, 2010).

ELL students may differ in their native languages, their level of English language and literacy skills, the length of time that the family has lived in the United States, their previous school experiences, their familiarity with school routines, their content-area knowledge, and their parental education (Rivera, Moughamian, & Francis, 2009). Each of these can impact on a student's literacy learning.

Understanding and Using Academic Language

Students in the tutoring program often can decode fluently but lack the skills of academic language and the complex grammar and background knowledge necessary to comprehend the text. Academic language is often referred to as the "language of school." Cummins (2000) defines academic language proficiency as "the extent to which an individual has commanded the oral and written academic registers of schooling" (p. 67). Becoming proficient in the use and understanding of academic language is essential for learning and success in school. Francis et al. (2006) note that "mastery of academic language is arguably the most important determinant of academic success for individual students" (p. 6). Academic language performs several functions: It explains, informs, justifies, compares, describes, persuades, and evaluates.

Students must be able to use and understand academic language in its various forms and purpose. Among them is the need to understand teacher explanations, to discuss what is being learned, to read for different purposes, to write about their learning, and to participate fully in the classroom. The expectations for students are high. They are expected to learn new words in context, determine the difference between relevant and less relevant information in school texts, and participate in student conversations related to text. This is often difficult for ELLs and struggling readers who have not yet developed language competence or do not have the background knowledge to understand the content presented.

Students often hear academic language from their teachers but do not have the opportunity to use it themselves. As a student gets older, the context of academic tasks becomes more cognitively demanding. It uses and requires comprehension of a variety of language forms for a variety of purposes, and it incorporates multiple language structures. New ideas, concepts, and language are often presented in a formal way through textbooks and teacher presentations, which can all occur simultaneously, providing students with little time to process and internalize the information presented. Because students rarely have opportunities to engage in dialogue using academic language, struggling readers (and particularly ELLs) have difficulty developing an understanding of academic language. (For a discussion of comprehending academic language in complex texts, see Chapter 7.)

When working with students whose levels of language competence and cultural and social backgrounds differ from the mainstream population, we believe that instruction should be multisensory, multifaceted, and engaging. It is critical to plan instructional activities that integrate multiple skills/strategies at the same time.

STRATEGIES FOR LANGUAGE AND LEARNING

Struggling students range in academic abilities and language proficiency. It is often difficult to determine if their difficulties result from lack of language proficiency or are related to specific facets of literacy. This is especially true when tutoring young ELLs who have to accomplish tasks in English at a time when they have not fully developed their native language. In most cases, it is not an "either, or" but, rather, a combination of language and literacy.

Given that language is central to learning, the remainder of this chapter will point out instructional techniques for tutoring that enhance language development for native and ELL struggling readers. The discussion first involves discourse and strategies that prepare students to participate effectively in a range of conversations that support comprehension and collaboration. Then it introduces PRC2 (Partnering for Content Literacy), an instructional model that supports students' language development and discourse, the integration and evaluation of new information, and ways to communicate information in a logical cohesive manner (Ogle & Correa—Kovtun, 2010). Finally, this chapter presents strategies to support sharing knowledge of ideas through listening and speaking.

Conversations and Discussions

Conversations are integral to communicate information, establish rapport, and share knowledge of ideas through listening and speaking. Conversation involves the use of language functions that express likes and dislikes, identify or describe, explain or clarify, and emotional responses that include wishing and hope, agreeing and disagreeing. Discussions are often more formal, thoughtful, and fact-based and involve the use of language functions that share facts, draw conclusions, evaluate ideas, choose solutions, rank opinions, or develop consensus. Conversations and discussions both are essential in developing language and are vital components in the tutoring session. Figure 6.2 presents a transcription of one of Alicia's tutoring sessions with her tutor Daniella. As you read it, what do you notice?

As demonstrated in the interaction between Daniella and Alicia, it is not easy to carry on a conversation or discussion when students do not have the academic vocabulary or background knowledge to respond quickly. As a tutor it is important to monitor the pacing of the discourse in the tutoring session and to incorporate wait time after questioning and throughout the conversation or discussion. When a tutor does not allow time for the

Figure 6.2. An Interaction Between Alicia and Her Tutor Daniella

TUTOR (DANIELLA)	STUDENT (ALICIA)
We've been working on our ladybug life cycle, and we finished our book. We are creating a picture representation of the life cycle for our newsletter. These are the things we are writing about. Pupa . . . we didn't finish writing about it. We are going to figure out the words that describe the pupa.	(1) Like a present
I want you to go into the text and find out about the pupa *(Daniella opens the book to the pupa page and gives the book to Alicia)*	
(1) In the text, how do the authors describe what a pupa looks like?	
Yeah, the text talks about how the pupa looks like it's wrapped up like a present. We talked about how it does not mean that it is really wrapped up with paper and a bow.	
What is that in the picture? (skin) How could we finish this sentence?	Skin
Why don't we come up with different ways of describing what we see? What are other ways we can describe the pictures of how it is wrapped like a present?	(Alicia does not respond)
(2) How could we explain why the pupa has a shell over it?	
What else could we say?	
What would you call this?	(Daniella points to the picture)

student to respond, the result is a one-sided conversation where the tutor "fires questions" at the student. It becomes more of a "gentle inquisition" than a conversation.

Daniella, an extremely capable tutor, looked closely at the transcript and noted in her daily reflection,

> I must become more aware of wait and think time. I need to remind Alicia to refer to her bookmark for talking points. I need to stop talking and allow her to take some ownership in her learning.

To prepare students to participate effectively in a range of conversations and discussions that support comprehension and collaboration, tutors have found the following strategies to be effective.

Thick-and-thin questions. The foundation for a good conversation is to avoid single-answer questions. The thick-and-thin questioning strategy is utilized to help students create questions pertaining to a text and to help students recognize the depth of the questions they ask. Alicia's tutor, Daniella, found the thick-and-thin questioning strategy to be beneficial for developing conversation by creating (thick) questions that generate ideas and foster conversation, as opposed to (thin) questions, which often result in one-word answers or limited discussion.

The following is an adaptation of McLaughlin and Allen's (2000) procedure to create thick-and-thin questions that will facilitate discussion and conversations in a tutoring setting:

1. Provide background and understanding for the terms "thick" and "thin."
   - ➤ Place two books on the tutoring table, one thick and one thin.
     - • Have student describe the thick object and the thin object.
   - ➤ Write the word "thick" on one index card and the word "thin" on a second index card
   - ➤ Have student read the words aloud and place the cards below the representative objects.
2. Introduce the thick-and-thin questioning strategy by telling students that they can use the thick-and-thin questioning strategy to generate discussion.
3. Explain the difference between thick questions and thin questions.
   - ➤ Thick questions deal with the big picture and large concepts and are open-ended.
   - ➤ Thin questions deal with specific content or words.

4. Model and guide the student to create thick-and-thin questions by providing stems for questions.
   - ➤ *Why, what if* for thick questions
   - ➤ *How, when, who* for thin questions

Formulate-share-listen-create. This is a variation of Think-Pair-Share (Johnson, Johnson, Smith, 1991a) that is beneficial in the tutoring setting. The procedure is as follows:

1. The tutor or the student asks a question. Both the tutor and the student *formulate* answers to the question individually.
2. The tutor and the student *share* their answer with each other.
3. The tutor models how to *listen* carefully to the student's answer. Then the student applies the same technique and listens to the tutor's answer. This is followed by a discussion of the similarities and differences in the answers.
4. Together the student and tutor *create* a new answer that incorporates the best of both responses.

Say something. Short, Harste, and Burke (1996) suggest stopping at certain points in a text, and asking students to take turns saying something. Struggling readers often view their reading task as they need to finish the assignment. They don't focus on the text or attend to their reading. "Say something" is a strategy that

---

In compliance with RTI (Response to Intervention), Victor, a sixth 6th-grade bilingual student, received 30 minutes of reading intervention per each day. He easily read short passages of grade-level text, answered multiple-choice comprehension, and participated in small-group discussion groups. Greg, Victor's tutor, noted that he was having difficulty understanding and discussing longer pieces of text. Greg decided to include the "Say Something" Strategy in the tutoring session. Vincent was asked to read aloud and, when signaled, Greg asked Victor to stop and say something about what he had read. Vincent's response was, "It was good." Greg realized that the "say something" directions were too vague and decided to include sentence starters in the process. First Greg modeled the "say something" strategy utilizing one of the following sentence starters:

- Make a prediction (I predict that or I bet that . . .)
- Make a comment (This is confusing because . . .)
- My favorite part so far is: Ask a question (What would happen if . . . *or* Do you think that . . .)
- Make a connection (This reminds me of. . . . The character made me think of. . . .)

Once Greg provided a scaffold and modeled the process, Victor actively participated in literacy conversations.

interrupts a reading to allow a student to think about what is being read and then discuss it with a partner or small group. This can be useful in the tutoring session, especially with students who have difficulty using language to process thinking and learning. It also helps to build collaborative conversations.

Tutors have noted that talking about text during the reading makes the process of comprehension more visible for the student, and "say something" is an excellent reading strategy to support discussion, comprehension, and active thinking.

A suggested procedure follows:

1. At some predetermined point in a text, the tutor and student stop reading.
2. The tutor asks the student to say something about what she is learning.
3. The student shares her thoughts with the tutor. The tutor responds, and they talk about the student's ideas.
4. They continue reading to the next stopping point and repeat the process.
5. At the end of the segment, the tutor considers the student's responses as to how she used language to process her thinking and learning. The tutor plans the next session to address any issues.

Partnering for content reading. Partner reading and content too (PRC2) is an instructional model that evolved from the work of Donna Ogle and Amy Correa-Kovtun (2010) in collaboration with a group of urban literacy coaches and university faculty to support English-Language Learners in social studies and science. In a classroom, during PRC2, partners with similar reading levels read short, informational texts. The students learn to preview and identify key features of the text and then read it together. They engage in oral reading, questioning and discussing, and then attend to important content vocabulary.

We have adapted the model for tutoring to promote fluid discussion and support oral fluency, silent reading, comprehension, and vocabulary learning. With implementation of the PRC2 instructional model, we noticed that tutors did less talking and the guided portion of the tutoring program became more interactive as the student and the tutor both engaged in purposeful conversation with a focus on academic vocabulary and higher-level thinking skills.

The tutors found that discussions provided them with information on students' misconception of the content. They were able to provide immediate feedback to the students and to embed academic language in an authentic setting that fosters the learning of vocabulary. Alicia's tutor, Daniella, found this to be a highly successful delivery model that supported Alicia's instructional goals.

The tutors commented that the PRC2 instructional model offers students deep engagement in the text, photos, and other text features, promotes discussion that emphasized finding evidence for ideas and opinions, supports each facet of reading content material by previewing text features, silent reading, oral reading, questioning, distinguishing important information from interesting information, making connections, identifying key vocabulary and, most important, promotes academic discourse in which students spend time "talking" and "sharing" their thinking and learning from the text.

Danielle commented that Alicia's oral communication, academic language, and vocabulary knowledge soared as a result of the in-depth conversations that ensued throughout PRC2, and also noted that as a result of multiple readings of the text, Daniella's oral and silent comprehension improved.

The following provides an overview of PRC2 in a tutoring setting.

> Caroline commented on how the PRC2 instructional model changed the quality and quantity of the discussion about text for Kiltae, 3rd-grade student, and Karlee, 6th-grade student. Both rarely spoke during the tutoring time, had difficulty sharing their ideas, and rarely smiled or contributed to the conversation. Once Caroline added PRC2 to the tutoring session, she commented on how the students' disposition as readers changed. "It was as if they became more 'alive' as readers. They certainly became more active and purposeful."
>
> The PRC2 model had a specifically strong impact on Kiltae. At the start of the reading program, he was extremely uncomfortable with reading in his head. He verbalized, "If I read in my head, I won't know the words." After three tutoring sessions in developing his comfort with the PRC2 routine, he clearly had discovered that he could read silently after all! Caroline believes he benefited from the silent reading and rereading and the oral reading that the PRC2 model offers. It was truly instrumental in promoting his transition from oral reading to silent reading.

1. **Select materials.** The tutor selects engaging quality content materials (trade books, magazines) matched to the students' instructional level that the student and tutor will share and read together.

2. **Preview the text.** Together, the tutor and student preview the text. Initially the tutor guides the student through the process of looking at the cover, table of contents, and through the book to point out text features and points of interest. Throughout this process, the tutor utilizes language stems to facilitate the discussion. For example:
    ➤ I think this book is about _____. What do you think the book is about?
    ➤ I can use text features to help me understand the text. These pictures tell me more about _____. What do you notice?
    ➤ I notice headings. The paragraph must be about _____. What do you think?
    ➤ I wonder if we will learn about _____. What do you want to learn about?
    Once the student has a clear understanding of how to preview the book, the student and tutor complete the text walk together.

3. **Choose the reading.** Together the tutor and student review the table of contents, select a chapter, turn to the representative page, and complete the first reading of the text.

4. **Complete the first read.** The student and tutor read both pages of the two-page spread silently. Following the first reading, the tutor asks if the student had encountered any unknown or difficult words in the text and discusses where needed.

5. **Complete the second reading.** For the second reading, the student and tutor decide who will read page 1 and who will read page 2 aloud. Each rereads silently the page that they will read aloud.

6. **Write a discussion question.** Initially, the tutor models and guides the student through how to write a discussion question. Following the second read, the tutor and student either choose a discussion question from a generated list of open-ended comprehension questions or write a question on a post-it note and place it in the book.
    We have found the following open-ended questions support ongoing conversation:
    ➤ Ask your partner a "who, what, where, when, or why question." Then have your partner ask you a "who, what, where, or why" question.
    ➤ Ask your partner what the main idea was. Now have your partner ask you what you think the main idea was. Support this with information from what you read.

➤ Ask for your partner's opinion of the piece. After your partner has provided an opinion, have your partner ask you, "What is your opinion?"

➤ Find something interesting in the text, and tell your partner what it reminded you of, then ask your partner to do the same.

6. **Read the page aloud to your partner.** The tutor reads a page to the student, then asks the student a question after reading aloud. The tutor and the student continue discussing the page that was read. The student reads the page to the tutor and follows the same procedure.

7. **Reflect on your learning.** The tutor models the reflection process. First the tutor shares one thing that he liked, questioned, or learned from reading the text. Then the student shares one thing that she liked, questioned, or learned from reading the text. Then the tutor shares what he learned about himself as a reader.

8. **Select vocabulary words.** The student adds four vocabulary words to the student's vocabulary notebook. To ensure that important, essential academic vocabulary is chosen, the tutor selects two words from the reading. This ensures that essential academic vocabulary is chosen. The student then selects two words to learn and adds to the student's academic vocabulary notebook. Students may use a representation of the word, a description of the word, the author's use of the word, or a personal use of the word as a reminder of the meaning.

When working with students who have not yet developed language competence or do not have the background knowledge needed to understand the content presented, a large portion of the tutoring time should integrate the content and include discussion. Tutors comment about the amount of time involved in utilizing the PRC2 model in the tutoring session but have found that is time well spent, as it incorporates oral and silence fluency, multiple comprehension strategies, vocabulary, and discussion.

> What I love most about the PRC2 model is that it promotes students to talk about text, to ask questions, and to explain their thinking. I believe this is so important for English Language Learners [ELL] and struggling readers. In participating in the PRC2 model, Kayleen is using new words, talking about new content, and explaining her thinking. I believe that when ELL students (or any students, for that matter) talk and verbalize their thinking and understanding about text and content, it deepens their understanding.

Vocabulary Building—Vocabulary Visits

Activities to build vocabulary are suggested in Chapter 5. In addition to those, we recommend the following, which are related to conversations and discussions.

- Preteach essential concepts and vocabulary using visual, kinesthetic multisensory methods to introduce the big idea rather than relying exclusively on language for understanding.
- Help students recognize and use cognates.

We particularly recommend vocabulary visits. The activity was developed by Blachowicz and Obrochta (2005) to engage students in a virtual fieldtrip with a content focus. Vocabulary visits begin with a scaffolded read-aloud of a text that broadens students' understanding of content. The tutor then uses a poster to reinforce important vocabulary, before reading more about the topic. The poster contains pictures of vocabulary related to the topic. Blachowicz and Obrochta have provided commercial materials on specific topics, but the concept of a virtual fieldtrip can be used with teacher-made materials.

The concept of the virtual fieldtrip is especially valuable for ELL students and students with limited academic vocabulary in the content presented. By having students match pictures and words and listen for words in the read-aloud, you can focus attention on academic language.

Rosa, a struggling fifth-grade ELL student currently failing social studies, has limited academic vocabulary and background knowledge on the U.S. government. To build background knowledge and vocabulary for the government study, Hally chose United States *Discovering the US* (Brannon, 2000). Hally conducted a text walk with Rosa. When Hally asked Rosa to talk about the picture that accompanied the text, Hally noted that Rosa did not recognize the picture and, therefore, was not able to see the relationship between the photographs and words. As a result, the text walk did not clarify the content but confused Rosa instead. The following day, Hally introduced the "implement the Vocabulary Visit strategy" during the partner/guided reading portion of the tutoring session (see Figure 6.3). Throughout her study of U.S. government, Rosa continued to add words to the poster, classified the identified words, and used the new vocabulary in her writing, reading, and conversations. We adapted the following procedure for vocabulary visits:

1. After reading the first text aloud, the tutor draws attention to the appropriate poster and introduces the goal of matching words to items on the poster.

Figure 6.3. Part of a Lesson Plan for Rosa

LESSON COMPONENT	STRATEGY/ACTIVITY
Partner/Guided Reading (20 mins) Expository	**Prereading**
Content: U.S. Government	Vocabulary fieldtrip
Text: *Government and Citizenship, Symbols of the United States*, Etta Johnson, 2007	Large poster of U.S. govt. 3 branches
	Rosa identified 3 words
Focus: Preview the text and build background knowledge of U.S. Government.	**Text walk** Rosa matched words to the poster throughout the text walk
Prereading Vocabulary fieldtrip—Text walk	**Vocabulary strategy** Discussed
Vocabulary: Picto-glossary	3 branches of government
New words: *court, congress, White House*	Content index card
	• Picture, word

2. The tutor models by saying, "When I look at the poster, I see a
   _____." The tutor write it on a post-it, then places the post-it
   on the chart. The student completes the same language stem:
   "When I look at the poster, I see a _____." Then the tutor
   writes the word on a post-it and place the post-it on the chart.
3. Together, the tutor and the student choose five or six words to post.
4. If desired, the tutor may introduce a second book on the same
   topic and add any new vocabulary to the poster when it is
   represented there.

Language Frames

Anchor Standard 6 of the CCSS for Speaking and Listening states that students will "adapt speech to a variety of contexts and communicative tasks, demonstrating command of formal English when indicated or appropriate." Native and ELL students need strategies to express themselves. The strategy of language frames can be an excellent support for conversation, academic vocabulary, and good discussion. Language frames are partial statements that represent the academic language and syntax required to communicate information. They provide students with a model and the means to use formal English.

In the exchange recorded in Figure 6.4, Daniella asked Alicia to describe what a pupa looks like. Alicia answered, "like a present." The conversation between Daniella and Alicia might have changed if she had had language frames for description to support her thinking (see Figure 6.4).

Figure 6.4. Possible Language Frames for Alicia

LANGUAGE FUNCTION	POSSIBLE SENTENCE FAMES	CUE WORDS
Identifying/ Describing Explaining	It has . . . It looks like . . . It feels like . . . It sounds like . . . It tastes like . . .	Use sensory words where applicable: looks feels sounds tastes smells
	The pupa has a shell over it because _____. The reason for the pupa to have a shell over it is _____.	is/is not/ because for example clarify make clear such as

When Daniella asked Alicia, "How could we explain why the pupa has a shell over it? What else could we say?" Alicia did not respond. Most likely, she would have responded if Daniella had modeled the use of the sentence frames for explanation in Figure 6.4.

Tutors have found that providing students with language frames allows the discussion to become more fluid. Depending on the language and the reading level, students reference language frames via a bookmark, an interactive posterboard, or an interactive word wall (listing function and cue words).

SAMPLE LESSON PLANS FOR ALICIA

A 4th-grade ELL, Alicia was reading at the 2nd-grade level with strong word recognition skills and oral reading rate. Although her oral reading rate was at the instructional level, she read word-by-word with little or no expression. She did not pay attention to punctuation or self-monitor when miscues interfered with her understanding of the passage. Her tutor, Daniella, planned each tutoring session to consist of five main parts: Fluency, Word Study, Partner/Guided Reading (PRC2), Writing, and Read-Think Aloud. Although Daniella addressed all components of the reading process, she placed an emphasis on discourse, academic vocabulary, and self-monitoring for oral reading accuracy. (See the sample lesson plans for Alicia in Figures 6.5 and 6.6.)

Figure 6.5. Lesson 8 for Alicia

Lesson Component	Strategies and Activities	Outcomes and Formative Assessment
Fluency (5–10 mins) **Reading familiar text:** "You don't look beautiful to me" DRA repeated reading passage **Level:** M **Time read:** 3 **WPM:** 114, 110, 98 **Accuracy:** 8, 9, 3	**Warm-up** Alicia read silently, highlighted "said," then read aloud Repeated reading 3rd reading Slow down for accuracy and correct reading of "said" Chart progress	"Warm-up was fun!" Alicia understood why it is important to highlight punctuation marks, and applied when completing repeated reading. Much improved, Will continue to do daily fluency warm-up to build prosody (expression) Repeated reading today Only error: substituted "say" for "said" 3 times but read "said" correctly 4 times. Continues to have difficulty with *say/said*. I think it's a result of ELL so decided to address when it comes up in reading, not make it a focus. Accuracy improved because of reduction in speed. At first she was disappointed that speed decreased, but took time to discuss importance of accuracy, that speed is not the goal. Need to model how to pace/monitor fluency and will continue to be a focus as she often reads too quickly and does not understand pacing.
Word Study: Print skill (10 mins) **Words their way level:** Within words **Focus:** *th/t* sound **Sight word:** said/say	Picture closed sort (*th*) sound—model, prompt, pronounce, sort Practice flashcards with focus on sight words said—Overlearning strategy Student read with various expression: whisper, loud, louder, slow, fast	**Closed sort:** Great job remembering pattern th/t. Time to move on to next pattern sort. Will begin with make a word, need to mix up word study more than sorting. Used overlearning strategy so she would read and reread "said" in multiple voices. Thought it would be more fun. She agreed and started to smile and laugh after reading the same words in many voices. She said, "I think I'll always remember the word SAID!" Will retest tomorrow and hope that it has finally "sunk in." If not, will address only when it comes up in text. (Time to move on!)

(continued)

Figure 6.5. Lesson 8 for Alicia *(continued)*

LESSON COMPONENT	STRATEGIES AND ACTIVITIES	OUTCOMES AND FORMATIVE ASSESSMENT
Partner/ Guided Reading (20 mins) PRC2 **Expository content:** Solar system **Text:** *Pluto, A Dwarf Planet,* Taylor-Butler, 2008 **Comprehension:** check for understanding/ retell **Vocabulary:** Review orbit, space **New words:** Pluto, spacecraft, surface	**Check for understanding** Read, cover, retell, reread Recheck and reread if needed **Summarize** Choose facts for KWL (learn) chart Fill in L in KWL chart **Vocabulary strategy** Review content cards Content index card Picture, personal definition	Alicia applied read, cover, retell / reread strategy independently, After each paragraph, we discussed the reading. Alicia highlighted with removable highlighter tape, identified one important fact and wrote "recorded" on sentence strip. Continued throughout the text. Alicia has made growth in determining importance as demonstrated in how she determined the most important information. She independently sorted sentence strips according to importance and chose to complete KWL chart. The sorting made sense, but she was not able to explain her rationale. Will continue to work on this concept. **Vocabulary** Much discussion ensued and noticed her discourse has also improved. Liked visualizing vocabulary so will continue to use in the tutoring session as it really helped her understood the word and write a "kid friendly" definition. Great improvement and continues to be an area for growth.
Writing (10 mins) Quick-write personal response: "What would it be like to travel to outer space"	**Strategy:** Show not tell	This was the first time that Alicia used this strategy. We took some time to talk about what life would be like to travel to outer space. I asked her to make a picture in her mind. She closed her eyes. When she opened her eyes she wrote down words that went with her vision, then wrote several sentences in response to the prompt. I explained that she could not use the words in the prompt. She included "travel" and "outer space" in her writing and lacked detail, sentence structure. Tomorrow we will reread her writing and revise to see if she can rewrite without using "travel" and "outer space." This was difficult. Might have her sketch or discuss before she writes.

LESSON COMPONENT	STRATEGIES AND ACTIVITIES	OUTCOMES AND FORMATIVE ASSESSMENT
Read-think-aloud (10 mins) **Narrative text:** *Sideway Stories from Wayside School,* Sacher, 1978.	**Strategy:** DLTA **Prediction:** Questions using academic language cues—student response full sentences & grammar focus	Alicia is really enjoying this portion of the tutoring session. She easily made predictions throughout the DLTA, but use of academic language was limited. Tomorrow will use sentence frames to guide the discussion.

Figure 6.6. Part of Two Sessions for Alicia

LESSON COMPONENT	STRATEGIES AND ACTIVITIES	OUTCOMES AND FORMATIVE ASSESSMENT
Session 10		
Partner/Guided reading (20 mins) PRC2 **Expository content:** Solar System **Text:** *Venus,* Simon, 1992 **Comprehension:** Determining important details **Vocabulary:** Review: orbit, space, Pluto, spacecraft, surface **New words:** poisonous, atmosphere	**Determining Important details** Wrote facts on sentence strips Divided into interesting and important **Summarize** Choose facts (important details) for KWL (learn) chart Fill in L in KWL chart **Vocabulary strategy** Review content cards Content index card • Picture, personal definition	Alicia is able to locate facts in her reading. Currently has 15 facts, so now have to determine importance. Had to spend extended time on concept of "interesting" and "important." This was quite difficult for her. Took time to discuss further to deepen her understanding of this difficult concept. Asked her to sort in 2 columns—interesting and important. She put all in the important column. Asked her why she placed all in important column and she responded, "Why did the author put them in the book if they are not important?" This took me by surprise. We will continue to talk about the difference between "interesting" and "important" as it is key for her to understand the concepts presented. This took more time than expected. Added two vocabulary cards and had her choose two cards to review.

(continued)

Figure 6.6. Part of Two Sessions for Alicia *(continued)*

LESSON COMPONENT	STRATEGIES AND ACTIVITIES	OUTCOMES AND FORMATIVE ASSESSMENT
Read-Think-aloud (10 mins) **Narrative text:** *Sideway Stories from Wayside School,* (Sachar)	**Strategy:** DLTA **Prediction:** Questions using academic language cues—student response full sentences & grammar focus	Before we began the read-aloud introduced two sentence frames. • I think that _____ will happen because _____. • I predict that _____ will occur because _____. Read several pages and asked Alicia to jot down her prediction. I did the same. Then I modeled responding in a complete sentence using one of the above academic sentence frames. Then Alicia did the same. She is beginning to understand answering in a complete sentence but does not fully understand how to support her thinking. Will continue to model and focus on this concept.
Session 12		
Partner/Guided reading (20 mins) PRC2 **Expository content:** Solar System **Text:** *Solar System,* Simon, 2007 **Comprehension:** Self-Monitoring Determining importance **Vocabulary:** Review *orbit, space, poisonous, atmosphere* **New words:** *mission, orbit*	**Self-Monitoring** Click/clunk strategy **Summarize** Choose facts (important details) for KWL (learn) chart Fill in L in KWL chart **Vocabulary Strategy** Review content cards Content index card Picture, personal definition	Introduced click/clack/clunk as a fix up strategy. Once I modeled, she began to understand why it was important to think about what to do when you hit a "bump in the road." Making a list to remind her of what to do when this occurs. Needs additional practice and modeling. Will continue to focus on this. Reviewed important and interesting. Today she was able to put in columns and explain why she chose each category. Was impressed with growth that she is making in determining importance. **Today:** Continue to revisit so she will be able to apply independently. **Vocabulary breakthrough:** When reviewing the words she asked if she could rewrite one of the important facts because she wanted to include the word "mission."

LESSON COMPONENT	STRATEGIES AND ACTIVITIES	OUTCOMES AND FORMATIVE ASSESSMENT
		We added the word in a different color ink. Will make sure that vocabulary cards are reviewed prior to writing interesting and interesting facts. Believe the time that we have been spending on discussion is of great importance and will continue not to rush the lesson and make sure time is allocated for rich discussion.
Read-Think-Aloud (10 mins) **Narrative Text:** *Sideway Stories from Wayside School* **(author?)**	**Strategy:** Visualization Using a mental image Chose to read aloud together	Alicia really enjoyed using visualization throughout the read-aloud. At the close of the session, she told me she knows exactly what the principal looks like because she listened to the words and made a picture in her mind. She used full sentences when she described the character. Will continue to incorporate visualization throughout the tutoring lesson as a scaffold to build language and vocabulary.

Things to Think About

1. Think of a time when a conversation turned into an interrogation. What occurred? What could you have done differently? Think of a time when a classroom discussion or guided lesson was all "teacher talk." How did it turn out? What would you have done differently? What could you do to avoid one-sided conversations in the tutoring session?

2. Try using one of the language stems found in Figure 6.4 with your students in relation to strategies you have taught them. Did it help to clarify the information? Did it help them to think metacognitively? How did it help you refine your instruction and thinking?

3. Think of occasions when you were not able to communicate because of a language difference? How did you communicate? Now think of a time when you spoke English and the majority of the group spoke a different language. How did you get your point across?

7 Comprehension of Text

Lisa was a 3rd-grade student who had trouble understanding extended pieces of text. When asked questions about the content of a sentence or a short passage, she was able to respond appropriately. Her school reported that her print skills were appropriate for her grade level, and that her general vocabulary knowledge was adequate. Lisa's teacher reported that when the class was engaged in discussion of a novel, Lisa found it hard to participate because of her lack of understanding. In addition, Lisa was struggling in social studies as a result of her comprehension difficulties.

Lisa's tutor, Andrew, confirmed that when Lisa was confronted with an extended passage or a book chapter, she was unable to make sense of what she was reading. Lisa understood that reading is about making sense but was not able to use this knowledge to gain appropriate meaning when reading. Andrew discovered, through diagnostic teaching, that Lisa was able to go back into text to find answers to questions but was unable to retell parts of a story or to find the main idea of a paragraph of expository text.

Lisa was like many struggling readers who are capable of many types of thinking in relation to their lives in and out of school. They make inferences, judgments, and moral decisions, weigh evidence, understand peoples' motives for their actions, and so forth. Yet, when it comes to text, these same capable thinkers struggle to comprehend. Some forms of comprehension occur in relation to subject matter, which students will not have experienced prior to school. After all, the purpose of education is to give students new lenses through which to view the world. Still, it is not uncommon to hear a teacher say, "My students don't know how to make inferences." Since even young children make inferences in their lives, what the teacher should be saying is that her students do not know how to make inferences *in relation to text*.

This chapter explores ways to help students such as Lisa develop better comprehension in relation to text. First it examines the importance of purpose in relation to reading, followed by a description of strategies to develop comprehension, to help students monitor their comprehension, and ways to scaffold their analysis of multiple texts. The chapter concludes with a closer look at new literacies and the implication of the digital revolution for students' learning in schools.

THE ROLE OF PURPOSE IN READING

We sometimes forget that all reading is purposeful. Even when reading the latest bestseller, we are reading with the purpose of enjoyment, which involves, among other things, reading to find out what will happen and monitoring our own enjoyment of the book and the events and characters in it. In school—although this is hopefully one type of reading that students do—they typically spend a lot of time reading to find information. Consequently, it is important that they understand how purpose affects what they do:

1. The purpose for reading governs the rate and depth of comprehension.
2. The purpose activates the plan for selecting information.
3. Readers should develop their own purposes if none is specified.

These all refer to what is sometimes called *flexibility* in reading. This means the ability to monitor reading to determine the extent to which the purpose of reading is being met, and to change reading behaviors when needed.

Understanding Academic Language in Complex Text

Many students in schools struggle with the academic language in school textbooks. Compare these two texts, both from middle-school books.

> His question was unfair because he knew that there was no possible choice—"my father" had to be the only answer. My father was a huge man who believed in things of the spirit, although my mother often maintained that the spirits he believed in came in bottles. (Cormier, 1998, p. 114)

> A peninsula is a piece of land nearly surrounded by water. The entire continent of Europe is a peninsula with smaller peninsulas jutting out from it. Because of these peninsulas, most places in Europe are no more than 300 miles from an ocean or sea. Its nearness to these bodies of water has influenced Europe in many ways. (Bednarz, Clinton, Hartoonian, Hernandez, Marshall, & Nickell, 2003, p. 327)

A struggling reader may not understand these two texts for many possible reasons. In the short-story example, the reader needs to understand two meanings of the word *spirit*, and to know that distilled liquids that can cause drunkenness are often sold in bottles. However, the structure of the text is fairly simple, even though the second sentence is 27 words long.

In contrast, the social studies text has much shorter sentences. Nevertheless, the process of nominalization means that the average noun-phrase is 4.2 words in length, and the longest is 7 words. These nominalizations repackage *processes* (normally expressed by verbs) and *qualities* (normally expressed by adjectives) into *things* (expressed in nouns) (Fang & Schleppergrell, 2010). As you read this paragraph, notice that it also has a fair amount of nominalization—one of the characteristics of academic texts.

In addition, in the social studies text, the first sentence is definitional (*peninsula*). Understanding the meaning of that sentence is necessary for a reader to comprehend the remaining part of the text. In addition, the reader may be left wondering about the difference between an ocean and a sea, and needs to recognize that the phrase "bodies of water" refers back to these words.

The tone of a short story is personal, in contrast to a social studies text, which is objective and impersonal. Much more could be said about the differing discourses of the content areas and the structures of academic language, but this is the basic point. As explained in Chapter 6, teachers sometimes think that they only have to teach the content of a subject area, and may focus on the main concepts, but vocabulary is not the only thing that causes difficulty for students. It also is the language—the nature of the discourse.

The Common Core State Standards (CCSS) in Reading elucidate anchor standards that are common across narrative and informational texts. Much emphasis is placed on reading complex text, close reading, and using evidence from the text in relation to responses. The CSSS notes that the complexity of a text is influenced by quantitative factors (such as sentence length and difficult words), qualitative factors (such as the subject matter), and reader variables. For many struggling readers these reader variables are significant in terms of text complexity. A text that might not be complex for readers who are on grade-level can be complex for struggling readers because they have not met the foundational standard concerning reading with accuracy and fluency for that particular text. Tutors may have to use texts that are below students' grade levels so they can read fluently and closely. In any case, they must be introduced to close reading that requires the type of engagement espoused by the CCSS and focus on finding evidence in texts for their ideas and opinions. The activities in this chapter are linked to certain standards in Figure 7.1. These are just examples, and many of the activities link to several standards.

Figure 7.1. Matrix of Activities Linked to Common Core State Standards for Comprehension

Foundational Standard

1   Read with sufficient accuracy and fluency to support comprehension.

Anchor Standards—Reading

1. Read closely to determine what the text says explicitly and make logical inferences from it: Cite specific textual evidence . . .

2. Determine central ideas or themes of a text. . .summarize the key supporting details and ideas.

3. Analyze how and why individuals, events, and ideas develop and interact over the course of a text.

5. Analyze the structure of texts . . .

6. Assess how the point of view or purpose shapes the content and style of a text.

7. Integrate and evaluate content . . .

9. Analyze how two or more texts address similar themes or topics . . .

FOCUS	ACTIVITY	EXAMPLE STANDARDS*
Close reading and analysis	DRTA QAR Annotation	Grade 2–St.1 Ask and answer questions such as who, what, where, when, why, and how, to demonstrate understanding. . .
		Grade 4–St.1 Refer to details and examples in a text when explaining what the text says. . .
Point of view	QtA	Grade 3–St. 6 Distinguish their point of view from that of the narrator or those of the characters.
		Grade 5–St. 6 Analyze multiple accounts of the same event or topic, noting important similarities and differences in the point of view they represent.
Analyzing structure	Focus on features, graphic representations, and clue words	Grade 3–St. 5 Use text features and search tools. . .to locate information relevant to a topic.
		Grade 5–St. 5 Compare and contrast the overall structure (e.g., chronology, comparison, cause/effect, problem/solution) of events, ideas, concepts, or information in two or more texts.
Central ideas and summarizing	3 important words GIST	Grade 4–St. 2 Determine a theme of a story, drama, or poem from details in the text; summarize the text.
		Grade 6–St. 2 Determine a central idea of a text and how it is conveyed through particular details; provide a summary of the text distinct from personal opinions or judgments.

(continued)

Figure 7.1. Matrix of Activities Linked to Common Core State Standards for Comprehension *(continued)*

Focus	Activity	Example Standards*
Integration and evaluation	Visualization Think-aloud checklist	Grade 1–St. 7 Use illustrations and details in a story to describe its characters, setting, or events.
		Grade 3–St. 7 Use information gained from illustrations and words in a text to demonstrate understanding . . .
Analysis of multiple texts	I-chart	Grade 2–St. 9 Compare and contrast the most important points presented by two texts on the same topic.
		Grades 4 & 5–St. 9 Integrate information from several texts on the same topic in order to write or speak about the topic knowledgeably.

The matrix is meant to show possible connections. Many activities apply to more than one standard. Each example represents the main focus of that standard. For example, Reading Standard 2 addresses determining central ideas or themes and summarizing.

*Example grade level standards are from the standards for literature and for informational text.

We want to emphasize that we conceive of reading comprehension as including many different forms of thinking in relation to text. Comprehension ultimately entails thinking about the information in text in complex ways that challenge students' ideas and biases. Even so, we should not lose sight of the fact that even struggling readers bring powerful thinking abilities to the reading situation but may not understand how to apply them.

Valuing Experiences of ELL Readers

Students living in our multicultural, multiethnic society come to school with a wealth of experiences. English Language Learners (ELL] comprise one group of students who bring diverse and valuable knowledge to the school setting, but these experiences do not always include knowledge that matches the demands of the school curriculum. As a consequence, literacy learning can be problematic because these students lack appropriate schemata to understand some of what they are reading. Therefore, it is essential that, we do not devalue the experiences and language knowledge that these students bring to reading and writing in English.

Compared to classroom teachers, tutors may have better resources and opportunities to match materials and instruction to the interests and knowledge of ELL students, partly because of the limited number of students with whom they work at any one time. It is important to consider that developing literacy skills is the primary purpose. Once students develop the abilities to be metacognitive in relation to their own literacy, they will be better able to deal with literacy in regular school settings. This is not to suggest that literacy instruction should be divorced from the regular curriculum. You should make as many connections as feasible within the context of motivation and appropriate instruction. This can be a fine line to draw, and only experience and careful monitoring will reveal the best way of working with each child.

Many tutors are not bilingual, yet find themselves working with a bilingual student. This is addressed somewhat in Chapter 6, but the issue is raised here because it is relevant to relating learning to existing knowledge and experiences. You must take care to develop strategies for comprehension while understanding the strengths and limitations of each child's prior learning.

STRATEGIES TO DEVELOP COMPREHENSION

You may be familiar with many of the strategies presented next. Still, the way they are presented can add to your understanding and facilitate your implementation in a tutoring situation.

Close Reading and Analysis

The first group of strategies requires close reading and analysis as part of the activity. Tutors should continue to emphasize the importance of textual evidence as students learn and apply the strategies.

Directed Reading Thinking Activity. Russell Stauffer (1969) introduced Directed Reading Thinking Activity (DRTA) with a substantial book. Our thinking is to keep DRTA as simple as possible, because students are more likely to make the transfer into their own reading. DRTA is a powerful tool for use with narrative text, and it places an emphasis on providing evidence for thinking about text. Students must learn that predictions are made and revised or discarded in relation to text, in much the same way as with films or videos. People often have multiple, and sometimes conflicting, ideas about what may happen in a story. This is one reason that the language of responding to predictions is important: They may be excellent predictions but not match the text. They are not "wrong" but may have to be modified or discarded in favor of a better idea.

Students need to understand that DRTA is an exercise to practice what readers do as they read—to hypothesize about what will happen. As such, you should spend time on determining or modeling the reason behind good predictions. The following outlines the procedure for using DRTA:

Preparation

1. Select a good story and do a story map of it, determining the characters, setting, problem, actions, and resolution in the story.
2. Determine four or five good stopping points based on the map— usually after the title, the setting (introduction of the characters, and maybe the initiating event or problem), the goal (the protagonist's response to the initiating event), the attempt(s), and the outcome (if there is a subsequent ending).
3. Avoid too many stopping points, and focus on points where new information will allow the modification of predictions.

The Lesson

1. Elicit from, or remind, the student(s) as to the rationale for the activity.
2. Elicit some predictions, and write them down. If you have more than one student, keep track of who made each prediction. Do not accept poor reasoning. Model as necessary. Probe as necessary.
3. Read *silently* to confirm, revise or discard the predictions (the wording is important—it is *not* to find if the predictions are *correct or incorrect*). Ask for evidence from the text to support the students' decisions.
4. Read the predictions, and confirm, revise, discard, or keep them. In a group, always ask the student who made the prediction. Physically mark them in some way.
5. Elicit new predictions and the reasons for them. Write down the new predictions.
6. Go back to procedure 4, until the story is ended.

After Reading

7. Talk about the story.
8. Review the purpose of the activity.

You may choose to use the story for further instruction—for example, for vocabulary work. Avoid making this an overly tedious use of one text.

Our experience with DRTAs tells us that there are several reasons DRTAs may not be effective or fail to engage the student(s):

- There are too many stopping points. Interrupting the reading of the story can ruin the "flow" and be frustrating if the readers are excited about finding out what will happen. Stopping every two pages is not an effective way of implementing a DRTA.
- The student's predictions are not based on the information in the text.
- The story is inappropriate for this activity. There has to be good structure to support the students' predictions. For DRTA, stories with surprise endings are not appropriate for teaching the value of making predictions. Although we enjoy reading them, and students do, too, if the ending is not predictable, the activity seems purposeless.

Lisa's tutoring lessons included DRTAs. Prior to tutoring, she was able to provide some predictions, but she often struggled to articulate why she had made these predictions. Her tutor, Andrew, spent several sessions modeling how to go back into the text to find reasons for predictions, and gradually released responsibility to Lisa as she became more competent.

Questioning—Question Answer Relationships. Two techniques in relation to having students ask questions are the Question Answer Relationships (QAR) and Questioning the Author (QtA). Many students with comprehension difficulties seem to be unable to pose good questions about what they have read. This is symptomatic of their passive role in reading but at times can take extreme forms. Some students, when asked to pose a question, just add a rising intonation to the end of a sentence from the text—"The penguins keep their eggs warm by putting them on their feet?"—rather than "How do penguins keep their eggs warm?" You might start students such as this at the sentence level using paired reading and the simple questioning technique, Question Answer Relationships.

Pearson and Johnson (1978) suggested classifying questions as follows:

- **Textually explicit**—the question has an answer stated in the text.
- **Textually implicit**—the answer requires integration of text information.
- **Scriptally implicit**—the answer must come from the reader's own knowledge base about the topic of the text.

Taffy Raphael (1984, 1986) translated this formulation into terms that elementary and middle-school students would find easy to understand—Question Answer Relationships. She chose four categories—Right There, Think and Search, Author and You, and On My Own. This categorization helps students understand that *both* information in a text *and* their existing knowledge are important in comprehension. The first two categories require students to use information from the text only, and the second two categories require that they use information they already know. This is the basic distinction that is essential during instruction, because the categories may overlap. Students do not have to correctly identify questions as belonging to a specific category (we might even disagree with each other on a given question), but students must be able to argue why they think a question or answer belongs in the chosen category.

Raphael suggests that *Right There* questions require a student to look for the information in a particular sentence. Often, words in the question may be included in the sentence. In tutoring this category, you might suggest that a student scan to find key words from a question. A *Think and Search* question requires students to put together information from different parts of the text (across sentences and/or paragraphs) to decide on an answer—commonly, then, to make an inference. In answering such a question, readers need to skim or reread for important information. An *Author and You* question requires readers to think about what they already know and how it connects with information in a text. This is also often an inference, but of a different order. Finally, *On My Own* questions can be answered without information from the story—just using things students already know about a topic or story. This last category is less emphasized in the CCSS, but it still may be important to solicit a reaction from students as to how they feel about a text.

The usual way for students to learn about Question Answer Relationships is for them to work with a text and specific questions about it and to classify those questions and find the answers. You might start with the basic distinction between information in the text, and information from prior knowledge. Once students are comfortable with *identifying* all four types or categories, they should begin to

Angel was a 5th-grade student reading at the 3rd-grade level. Her print skills were above grade level, but she struggled to make sense of text, especially expository passages. Her tutor, Melanie, asked her to read various articles from the National Geographic *Pathfinders* series. These magazines have short paragraphs about interesting topics. Each session, Angel chose a new topic, and then she and Melanie read a paragraph silently and took turns asking each other questions using the QAR framework. After seven sessions doing this, they moved into more extended text to allow Angel to practice what she had learned.

formulate each type of question. In tutoring, this can be best achieved by taking turns to ask questions. Thus, instead of using the question words, you might say "I'm going to ask you a *Think and Search* question. What do ___?" After students locate an answer, you can specify the type of question to answer: "Let's read on to the end of the next paragraph, and then I want you to ask me an *Author and You* question." It is important to preview a text so you know that you can formulate an appropriate question at your chosen stopping points. This avoids making the mistake of asking students to formulate a type of question and then realizing that you cannot think of one yourself!

Finally, remind students how using QAR categories can help them understand a text and answer questions about it. The goal is to have students be active readers and to be metacognitive about their own learning. Useful materials in this regard can be found at http://www.readinglady.com/mosaic/tools/QARQuestionAnswerRelationshipTeachingChildrenWheretoSeekAnswerstoQuestions.pdf

Point of View—Questioning the Author

A strategy developed and expanded by Beck and McKeown (2006), Questioning the Author (QtA), requires students to read texts closely to determine why the authors wrote them the way they did. The basic premise is to make explicit that readers should try to understand what the author was attempting to convey by asking questions such as "What is the author trying to say?" and "Why do you think the author uses the phrase....?" Strengths of QtA are helping students to recognize the depth of information that a text may provide (whether narrative or expository) and to recognize the fallibility of authors of informational text. The emphasis on the author and the text requires a student to approach texts from differing perspectives, and to take on different points of view.

As with most tutoring, it is important to select a passage that is both interesting and can spur a good conversation. This may be either narrative or expository, although Beck and McKeown (2006) argue that QtA may be best suited to nonfiction texts. Once a text is selected, you have to decide appropriate stopping points where you think your students need to obtain greater understanding. For each of these stopping points, you need to create appropriate questions (queries), such as those suggested above. Follow-up questions might be:

> For informational texts, "Does the author explain this clearly?"
> With a narrative, "Knowing what we do about this character, what do you think/he is doing now (or will do)?" "How has the author let you know that something has changed?"

Model for students how to answer questions such as these.

Beck and McKeown (2006) make explicit some discussion moves that a teacher or tutor can make in developing students queries and answers:

- **Marking** may draw attention to an idea.
- **Turning back** asks students to go back to the text to find information to clarify a response.
- **Revoicing** is when the tutor rephrases a question that a student has asked.
- **Modeling** may go to the text to show how to find ideas that were missed.
- **Annotating** is where a teacher provides context—information that students may not have that helps comprehension.
- **Recapping** pulls ideas together or summarizes what has been understood.

These discussion moves may be familiar to you in your own teaching, but sometimes it helps to have our own pedagogy made more explicit and named. Further information and examples may be downloaded from http://www.readingrockets.org/strategies/question_the_author?theme.

QtA develops comprehension on differing levels without being specific about the nature of the comprehension processes used. You can help develop comprehension in an area where a student is struggling, whether it is with inferential comprehension, or with summarizing, or for any other need.

Once Lisa became comfortable with asking questions, Andrew introduced QtA by modeling his thinking in relation to instructional level text. He was surprised when Lisa seemed to understand taking this approach to text. He wrote:

> Lisa seemed to find this easier than when we began QAR, but I think it is because we laid a good foundation. After two sessions, when we paused our reading the first time, she said, "I think the author is trying to tell us…" without any prompting. I'm so proud of her. She's becoming a more active reader and starting to find her way around a text.

Example lesson plans for Lisa using some of these strategies are at the end of the chapter—Figures 7.8 and 7.9.

Analyzing Structures

We are always surprised that students in the middle grades can still have difficulty using the macrostructure of a textbook. After they have been in school several years, you would expect them to understand the function of headings and subheadings, of bold words, of illustrations and captions, and of other types of graphics. But often, struggling students in the elementary and secondary grades still fail to use these aids to comprehension. One of the reasons for the failure is a lack of understanding about the functions they serve. In general, students do understand the contents page, the glossary, and the index—that is, they understand how to use them, even when they commonly don't use them. It is a good idea to check their understanding of these elements.

"Attack the Title." One method of coordinating all of these text features comes from Betsy Niemiec and her primary-grade students. They developed a way of remembering to use the features by linking the strategy to the alphabet and came up with six mnemonics:

> **Attack** the Title—look and think what it means
> **Be** aware of the **Bold** Words
> **Capture** the **Captions**
> **Determine** the Main Idea—look for repeated words in the paragraph
> **Examine** the Illustrations, Charts, and Graphs
> **Fish** for the **Facts**

Betsy says that the power of using the alphabet is that the students themselves thought of the word for each letter. Other teachers and tutors have said that kids have used the mnemonic as it is, and like that other students have thought of it. Either way, it utilizes text features to help students read textbooks effectively. You might think of other mnemonics—perhaps you can work out what THINK could stand for.

Interestingly, when Lisa's tutor, Andrew, asked her to look at a simple nonfiction text, which was at an independent level for her in terms of her print skills, she was able to identify the contents page, the headings and subheadings, and the captions for the illustrations. But she could not articulate how knowing these elements could help her read the text successfully, or to actually use them to aid her understanding. Andrew reported that it was not difficult, once she had become an active reader in narrative text, to help her use text features to scaffold her comprehension.

Text structures. Writers of informational texts organize information in several ways. The different internal organizational patterns of these texts are commonly:

> description (main ideas and details)
> sequence of events (or time order)

comparison/contrast
cause and effect
problem/solution

Various graphics have been developed to make these organizational patterns more easily understandable. Some of these are shown in Figure 7.2.

Figure 7.2. Five Macro-Structures in Expository Text

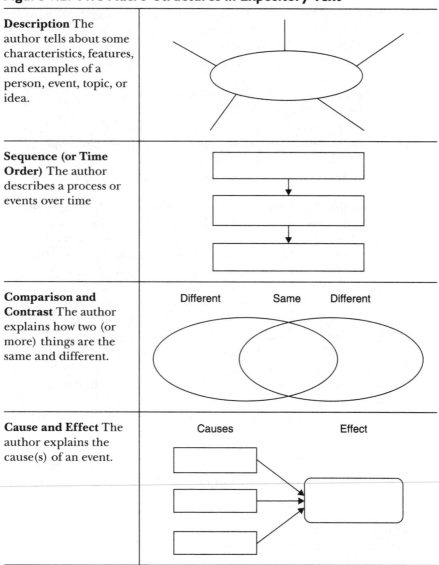

Description The author tells about some characteristics, features, and examples of a person, event, topic, or idea.	
Sequence (or Time Order) The author describes a process or events over time	
Comparison and Contrast The author explains how two (or more) things are the same and different.	Different Same Different
Cause and Effect The author explains the cause(s) of an event.	Causes Effect

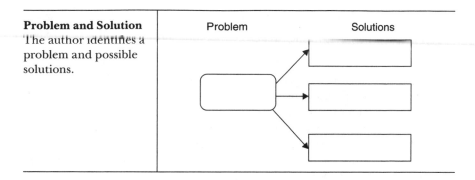

Problem and Solution
The author identifies a
problem and possible
solutions.

One way to help students understand these patterns is to have sample texts that exemplify the patterns for practice. The Internet is a good source for short informational texts with identifiable patterns. Once students are comfortable identifying the patterns in texts you provide, they can move on to identifying them in textbooks and other materials. In addition to graphic organizers, providing students with a list of words commonly used in the various patterns can help them recognize how the author has organized the ideas (see Figure 7.3).

As a caution, the various patterns can be embedded within each other. For example, the main organization of a passage could be sequence, but within that, some information could be cause and effect. If students initially find identifying patterns to be fairly easy, it may be worth spending extra time to identify such embedded text structures. However, some students find that recognizing text structures is not helpful in their studying, and time may be better spent on other ways to learn from text.

Figure 7.3. Words That May Help in Identifying Text Patterns

SEQUENCE/ TIME ORDER	CAUSE-EFFECT/ PROBLEM-SOLUTION	COMPARE-CONTRAST
After	Accordingly	Also
Before	As a result of	But
Finally	Because	Conversely
First, second, etc.	Consequently	Either ... or
In the past	Due to	However
Initially	Eventually	In comparison
Later	If ... then	In contrast
Next	Since	Not only ... but also
Now	Subsequently	Yet
Following	Therefore	
	Thus	

A good way to help students apply their knowledge of text organization is to have them write passages that demonstrate the structures they have studied. Initially, you might provide students with information in one of the graphic forms and have them convert that information into regular text. Once they become facile with these forms, ask them to use these in their own informational writing.

If you have taught students a note-taking strategy, you might consider showing them how you can use the organizational patterns in text to take more effective notes. This can be done by including one of the graphic organizers within the note-taking format. A useful tool for note-taking using electronic media is Evernote: http://evernote.com.

Central Ideas and Summarizing

One of the hardest tasks for struggling readers is to teach them how to summarize. The GIST game-like activity might be helpful.

GIST. GIST is a strategy that often works best initially with a group, but it also has been used successfully in individual tutoring. GIST helps students work interactively with informational text to write brief summaries. It develops comprehension and summarizing skills by asking them to be selective in their word choice. The basic idea is to force students to write the *gist* of a paragraph/passage in 15 words. Following is the GIST procedure:

1. Select an appropriate passage—three to five paragraphs in length. Prepare copies for all the students.
2. Read the initial paragraph together. Put 15 blank lines on the board. Model for the students how to summarize the paragraph in 15 words. Model how to make initial attempts that can be modified by erasures and substitutions.
3. Put up 15 more blank lines. Read the second paragraph together. Now have the students suggest how to complete the blanks to summarize the next paragraph.
4. Have the students work individually to generate 15 word summaries for subsequent paragraphs. Ask them to share and write some on the chalkboard. Praise all the attempts, and show how all the ones you wrote on the board are good summaries, even though they are different.

Ask students to use their paragraph summaries to make a final summary for the whole passage.

Three important words. As another strategy to help students identify main ideas in expository text, and to write summaries, ask them to identify three important words in a paragraph (Hoch, Bernhardt, Schiller, & Fisher, 2013). The idea of identifying important words as a clue to main ideas is not new (Cunningham & Moore, 1986; Yopp & Yopp, 2007), but it is a good strategy because it seems easy for students and gives them a doable process. A lesson might be as follows:

1. Break the text into short manageable sections—perhaps use each paragraph.
2. Model how to select three words that represent the main idea(s) of the paragraph, write them on a post-it note, and stick the note next to the paragraph in the book. Give reasons why these words were chosen.
3. Have students continue to the end of the text (with support), and then review the words.
4. Provide some graphic organizer that helps the students organize the words into meaningful groups. Have the students write a sentence about each grouping of words.
5. Use the sentences to construct a summary of the text.

Modeling word selection is vital. Here is an example of a think-aloud to model the process, pertaining to Chinese immigration:

> The Chinese also found other jobs in the United States. They worked as cooks, servants, carpenters, and laborers. By the mid-1850s, the gold had almost run out. Miners returned from the mines to go back to their old jobs. When they could not find work, they blamed the Chinese for taking the jobs. Soon, people began to blame the Chinese for anything that went wrong. (Dickson, McGuire, & Shymansky, 2007, p. 12)

After reading the passage aloud you might say:

> The information in this paragraph is all very interesting—like how the Chinese were blamed for everything. That seems to be one of the main ideas, so one of my words is *blame*. The author introduces the paragraph by talking about how the Chinese took all kinds of jobs, and then tells me some of them. I think it is important that the Chinese were blamed first for the loss of jobs, so my second word is *jobs*. Hmmm, let's see. For my third word, I could choose *miners* because they were the ones who came back and found their jobs taken. Or I could choose *gold* because it happened when the gold ran out. I think either would work, but I'm going to use *minors*.

Having modeled the process, you can support students as they try it with subsequent paragraphs, and then scaffold the work of constructing a summary for the entire text. Andrew tried this method with Lisa, and she found it helpful.

Selecting three important words can be seen as a form of annotation. Another purpose for annotating is given below.

Annotating texts. You may have had the experience of looking at a student's book or material copied for studying in which most of the text is highlighted (often in yellow, for some reason). Students should be encouraged to move away from highlighting to some other form of "annotation," simply because it reflects an inability to select relevant information, and to understand the necessity for processing different parts of texts in varying ways. A good system of annotation can help students stay focused and involved with their textbooks. The following gives some techniques that students can use to annotate text:

1. Underline important concepts and terms.
2. Circle definitions and meanings.
3. Write key words and definitions in the margin.
4. Use words or symbols in the margin to indicate where important information is located.
5. Write short summaries in the margin where appropriate.
6. Write questions in the margin next to the section where the answer is found.
7. Indicate steps in a process by using numbers in the margin.

Not all students are allowed to mark textbooks, so you should provide students with materials on which they can annotate in this way. Any system of annotation can be adapted to use with post-it notes. As with all instruction, careful modeling is necessary when teaching students to annotate. A useful tool for annotating online text, free to educators, can be found at www .diigo.com.

Integration and Evaluation

Too often, students who are struggling do not recognize that strategies taught to them have to be integrated, not used in isolation. Integration of strategies and integration of content in a text have some commonalities, with the underlying assumption that the goal of reading is to make meaning of text.

Think-aloud checklist. Once students have learned some ways of interacting with text, it may be appropriate to engage in a think-aloud to demonstrate how the strategies work together. Too often, tutors engage in a think-aloud and the students sit there looking puzzled because they have no idea what they are supposed to be observing. One way around this is to provide them with a Think Aloud checklist (Niemlec & Hess, 2007). A possible version may look like the one in Figure 7.4.

Figure 7.4. Think-Aloud Checklist

Instruction: Put a tally mark next to the strategy each time you hear me use it as I think aloud about my reading:

STRATEGY	TALLY
Setting a purpose for reading	
Predicting	
Summarizing	
Questioning	
Visualizing	

After giving students the checklist, read a text aloud, stopping at various points to think-aloud, using one of the strategies the students have learned. Instruct the students that when they recognize a strategy, to put a checkmark in the space in the Tally column for that strategy. Students initially may need prompting to fully understand the task. Once they have done so, the tutor and the students can reverse roles; the students think aloud while the tutor checks the list. This is a good way to show students which strategies they use most often, and to remind them of all the ways in which they can engage effectively with text.

Visualization. Another way to teach integration is through visualization. The process of visualizing what is happening in a text requires integration of content, although students may not be aware that this is what they are doing. A necessary component of reading comprehension is the reader's ability to create mental pictures based on the text. Unfortunately, too many struggling readers read word-by-word and do not make sense of what they are reading because they fail to integrate the information in a meaningful way. Students such as these benefit from being taught to visualize as they read—especially with narrative texts and plays.

Visualizing strengthens reading comprehension as students consciously use the text to create mental images. With even limited practice, the act of visualizing text can become automatic. Students who visualize can comprehend more and can recall what they have read for longer periods of time (Harvey & Goudvis, 2007).

The basic process of tutoring for visualization is to begin with small amounts of text, model, and then have students create their own images.

One idea is to make connections to films—to think of being a director and deciding how to translate what is in a book into images on a screen. Make clear that different directors may interpret the same text in different ways. In addition, in regard to reading, emphasize that a reader may start out with a specific image—perhaps one that is not very well developed— and add to and change it as the author reveals more information. A series of short exercises can develop the student's ability to visualize and allow transfer to regular text quickly. Two of these exercises are included as Figures 7.5 and 7.6 (Fisher & Polkoff, 2003).

Figure 7.5. Visualization Exercise 1

The man walks slowly into the yard carrying a shovel and a cardboard box.

In which hand is the shovel? What is he wearing on his feet?

He walks slowly, with his head bent. No sound disturbs the stillness except the thud of his boots on the earth and the uneven hiss of his breath.

What time of year is it? How old do you think he is?

He stops briefly several times as he walks to shift the box from one arm to the other, resting the shovel against his side as he does so.

What can he see if he looks around him? Is the sun shining?

Eventually the man stops by an empty vegetable plot. He takes out a large handkerchief and noisily blows his nose.

What color is his handkerchief? Which pocket does he take it from?

Slowly he begins digging a hole, piling the heavy wet earth to one side. Every third or fourth shovelful he stops and holds his back.

How big is the hole he is digging? Which side of the hole is the earth piled?

Finally he rests. He puts down the shovel and places the box slowly in the center of the hole. He bows his head as it begins to rain.

What was in the box? Why is the man bowing his head?

Figure 7.6. Visualization Exercise 2

Katie holds up one finger to test the wind. The strong breeze rustles the leaves of the large trees at the park.

What time of year is it? How old is Katie? What is Katie wearing?

She opens a plastic bag. She reads the directions slowly and begins to assemble the large dragon. After putting it together she tests the string to be sure it will hold.

What color is the dragon? Where is the string attached to the dragon? How does she test the string?

Katie walks toward the large open space and the long tail of the dragon begins to unfurl behind her. The wind pulls at the dragon and it begins to fly.

What is the dragon? How long is its tail?

Katie dashes into the field heading straight into the wind. The dragon soars behind her. As the string bites into Katie's hands she can feel the force of the wind.

Is Katie wearing gloves? Are there other children doing the same thing as Katie?

Suddenly the kite stops. It is no longer pulling new string from Katie's hands. She pulls on the string but cannot bring the kite down. The tail flaps in the breeze. Katie drops the roll of string next to her and it does not move. She sits down in frustration and covers her eyes with her hands.

Where is the kite? What expression does Katie have on her face? What does the tail look like now?

With these exercises reveal a segment of text to the student. We recommend having the student move an index card down the printed text to expose each new segment. After the student reads each piece of text, the tutor asks, "What do you see?" When the student gives a description, you can pose the extra questions to help develop the image that the student has created. You may find that these exercises show some cultural bias. For example, it would be hard for students who have never flown a kite to complete the exercise in Figure 7.6. Consider constructing your own exercises that relate to situations that are familiar to your students, or even encourage students to construct them for each other. Here is a guideline for how to go about doing this:

1. Choose a setting and an experience that is well known to the students.
2. Think-through a sequence of events in your own head, visualizing each moment.
3. Choose a sequence that allows for some ambiguity. Ensure that the first item allows for multiple interpretations and the ambiguity is gradually resolved.
4. Write each of the five to six stages of the sequence in one to three brief sentences.
5. Try it out by having someone else (or even more than one person) read the sequence, gradually showing each item.
6. Write two or three questions to induce imagery for each item.

As you develop questions for each segment of text, you may find it useful to consider Nanci Bell's (1991) 12 structure words that she suggests using to prompt students to make better images: *what (do you see?), size, color, number, shape, where, movement, background (around), perspective, when, sound, mood.*

After engaging with three or four of these exercises, students usually are ready to try visualizing with longer segments of real text. You will have noticed that to create images, readers need to combine their background knowledge with information from the text, and to make inferences. Once students have become facile with visualization, it may be appropriate to point out this process and how it applies in all reading situations.

Some authors recommend having students draw pictures to develop the ability to visualize. This sometimes can work effectively, but drawing pictures tends to place limits on the idea of visualizing while reading. Readers must have a fluid image, which may change and be altered as more information comes available. In our experience, students are reluctant to alter a drawing once they have made it. This solidification at a certain point in the text may work against better comprehension later.

STRATEGIES TO MONITOR COMPREHENSION

You may teach students comprehension strategies, and they may be proficient at using these when prompted, but students do not necessarily use these strategies when comprehension breaks down. It is hard to teach students to be metacognitive and to monitor their own understanding. However, the "Click and Clunk fix-up" strategy, the "Important and Interesting Facts" strategy, and the "Train Your Brain to Read Bookmarks" strategy have been effective with struggling readers.

Click and Clunk Fix-Up Strategy

In the Click and Clunk strategy, the words that students instantaneously read and understand are called *clicks*. The words that make no sense to them and interfere with fluency and comprehension are known as *clunks*. Clunks are like potholes in a road that hinder the process of smooth driving. Students use the strategy to "fix-up" their understanding and clarify the meaning of the clunk. The tutor models the strategy when reading a passage orally at the student's instructional level. The lesson might proceed as follows:

1. The tutor explains the difference between a click and a clunk: "You are riding your bike on a smooth sidewalk (clicking away), then you hit a bump (clunk)."
2. The tutor reads while the student follows in the text. When the tutor hits a clunk (reads a word incorrectly), the student reports

the clunk. The tutor models and "thinks aloud" what to do after hitting a clunk.

> ➤ Reread the sentence without the clunk.
> ➤ Substitute another word that might be appropriate in place of the clunk.

3. The tutor continues to model by reading the sentence before the clunk, rereading the sentence with the clunk, and reading the sentence after the clunk, while looking for clues to help figure out the clunk:

> ➤ words or phrases that may support the meaning of a clunk.
> ➤ clues in "Chunk the clunk," while looking for a prefix or suffix in the clunk that may help to define its meaning.
> ➤ smaller, more familiar words that are part of the clunk that may support the clunk's meaning.

4. The student tries to implement the strategy independently or with a paired reading.

Important and Interesting Facts

Successful readers are able to determine important versus unimportant details when reading informational texts. Being able to sort important facts from the less important facts is a critical skill in developing deeper understanding in content-area reading.

ELLs and struggling language students often categorize all details as important. When introducing and modeling the important/unimportant reading strategy, the students often still have difficulty identifying important information. One tutor, Susie, asked a student, Alejandro, to explain his thinking. Susie discovered that he did not understand the term "unimportant." He thought that if it was in the text, "it had to be important."

In this case, we decided to change the term "unimportant" to "interesting." Once the categories were changed to "important" and "interesting," Alejandro was able to distinguish between important and interesting facts and then identify important facts as related to key ideas and themes in the reading. Tutors should use informational text at a student's instructional level with supporting text features and should have some blank strips of paper on which to write sentences. The procedure is then as follows:

1. The tutor reads one or two paragraphs of the text orally as the student follows along. The student can review the pictures/words during or after the initial reading.
2. Following the reading, the tutor or the student writes facts/details from the text on sentence strips—one fact per sentence strip.

3. The student sorts the facts/details into two piles with the tutor's support: i. Important; ii. interesting. They discuss reasons why the facts are important or interesting.
4. As the student becomes more proficient, the tutor may add a third pile for unimportant facts.

Comprehension Bookmarks

Bookmarks focus students' attention on specific comprehension strategies, thus strengthening their understanding of the process taught. Adding graphic and language stems encourages independent use of the strategy. The tutor and student together may want to design a bookmark to provide a visual cue to clarify the process and help the student think metacognitively. What is on the bookmark depends on the strategies that a student has been taught. Useful materials on bookmarks can be found on the Internet. Here are two websites:

> http://www.sanjuan.edu/webpages/gguthrie/resources.
>   cfm?subpage=122409
> http://www.bainbridgeclass.com/comprehensionbookmarks.pdf

ANALYSIS OF MULTIPLE TEXTS: USING AN I-CHART

More and more frequently, students are being asked to use a number of sources of information to investigate a given topic. Hoffman (1992) devised the Inquiry Chart (I-Chart) to help students work to collect and synthesize information from various sources. This I-Chart is particularly useful when students use the Internet to collect information from various websites. Although there is no definitive format for an I-Chart, it normally includes several components—what we know, questions, at least three sources, summaries or syntheses of the information from the different sources, interesting facts, and new questions. A completed I-Chart on Irish immigration is shown in Figure 7.7.

David was a 6th-grader who was a grade-level below in his reading ability for both print skills and comprehension. He was on a baseball team and liked to read about baseball. Jennifer, his tutor, used various magazine articles to develop his comprehension processing of multiple texts, using an I-Chart. Over 16 sessions, he made three charts about different topics—the Cubs, the All-Star game, and Jackie Robinson. David learned to ask good research questions, and to integrate information from across several texts.

Figure 7.7. A Completed I-Chart on Irish Immigration

Topic	What We Know	Source 1	Source 2	Source 3	Summary
Immigration		www.america.gov	www.historyplace.com	www.loc.gov	
Question 1 Why did Irish immigration slow down?	We know it spiked in the 1850s as a result of the potato famine. Then we know it decreased	During the 1850s, that's when the potato famine stopped	Civil War, hostile American environment	The potato fungus was found and destroyed	During the Civil War, the potato famine stopped; hostile American environment
Question 2 What kind of work did Irish immigrants do?	Hard labor; unwanted jobs	Unskilled, low-wage jobs	"Back-breaking work"; railroad work	They dug canals	Unskilled, low-wage jobs; back-breaking
Question 3 What challenges did they face?	Lack of money; disease	They rented farms and did not own. They lost their homes and farms. They were starving. Travel was difficult.	Religious prejudice of protestant masters to the Catholic Irish Political subordination	Greedy men forced them into tenements and extracted outrageous fees.	The challenges include but are not limited to lack of money, disease, religious persecution, etc.
Interesting facts		Irish Americans ended up holding a lot of power within communities.	JFK was the first Irish and Catholic President	St. Patrick's Day is not celebrated in Ireland the way it is in the United States	
New questions	How is the Irish experience of immigration similar to other immigrant groups?	Are people from Ireland still immigrating to the USA. If so, how many?	How do the Irish in Ireland view Irish-Americans?		

153

The process for using an I-Chart is as follows:

1. Students think about what they know about a topic, and develop three questions. Prior to developing the questions they want to investigate, the students might read an easy passage about the topic.
2. Once the questions are chosen, the students try to find appropriate sources, or the tutor chooses some sources to search (or guides students to sources).
3. Students make notes of specific information from each source that provides an answer to one or more questions.
4. Once all the information has been identified, students write a summary answer for each question.
5. Students can return to the "texts" to note other interesting facts or surprising information.
6. Students then pose new questions in which they are interested.

I-Charts can be a way to teach students to integrate information from a variety of sources. They require close reading of complex texts to answer meaningful questions, and thus offer an exceptionally useful way to include many of the Common Core State Standards in instruction.

NEW LITERACIES

The nature of literacy is undergoing profound change as access to the Internet in the United States becomes almost universal and people become familiar with using the Internet as a source of information. Students use email and instant messaging, download music, shop on the Internet, surf the Internet for information, engage in complex virtual games, and are part of social networks. Students may be avid and comfortable users of technology for a variety of purposes, but little of what they are doing is academic work, and most is performed outside school (Grisham & Wolsey, 2006). The term "new literacies" refers to the ability to interact with text in a variety of forms, but often specifically refers to using the Internet to access and communicate information.

There has been a paradigm shift in the conception of what it means to be literate. In a "post-typographic" environment, literacy means engaging with various forms of text, including, for example, hyperlinks, films, semiotic languages, three-dimensional worlds online, chat spaces and blogs, and emoticons used in email and on social networks.

Although online and offline reading comprehension require many of the same skills, these new literacies of online reading comprehension also require the ability to accurately identify, locate, critically evaluate, synthesize, and communicate information (Leu, Zawilinski, Castek, Banerjee, Housand, Liu, 2007). Because tutors have an obligation to facilitate students' learning in all environments, it is important that they know their students' task demands related to online reading. Being able to synthesize information may be a common factor between online and offline reading comprehension, but the other four of Leu's categories are specific to the Internet and new technologies (if communicating means engaging in multimedia presentations, for example).

When engaged in online reading, students must be purposeful. They need to be able to solve problems and find the answers to questions. Some of the purpose-setting strategies described in this chapter (such as an I-Chart) can be useful in this regard. In addition, as a result of the technology, readers can each create their own combination of texts, depending on which links and websites are chosen. Such online reading, then, demands that we tutor students about the importance of evaluating various sources of information, a new skill. Further, we have to tutor them in how to use that information to communicate what they have learned, using a variety of formats and media. The Common Core State Standards recognize the importance of this in the Grade 7–12 standards:

> **Reading Standards for Informational Text, Integration of Knowledge and Ideas, Standard 7, Grades 11–12.** Evaluate the advantages and disadvantages of using different mediums (for example, print or digital text, video, multimedia) to present a particular topic or idea.

Each student and each tutoring situation is unique. Younger students may not need instruction and guidance in using the Internet for academic purposes. Older students may be limited by their access to the appropriate technology. Increasingly, however, it will become necessary to articulate and evaluate the skills necessary to be an effective online reader. Leu, Coiro, and their colleagues (Coiro, 2011; Coiro & Castek, 2010; Leu, Kinzer, Coiro, Castek, & Henry, 2013) and the Program for International Student Assessment (http://nces.ed.gov/surveys/pisa/) have begun to articulate what an online reading comprehension assessment might look like. As literacy tutors, it is important to consider this work and how it might influence your students.

SAMPLE LESSON PLANS FOR LISA

Lisa was a 3rd-grade student whose print skills were at grade level. She needed to work on reading for meaning in both narrative and expository text. In oral reading, her miscues maintained meaning at the sentence level, so she was monitoring her comprehension of short pieces of text. However, she was unable to answer questions about extended text, suggesting that she was a "passive" reader, who did not actively engage with the content of what she was reading. Figure 7.8 gives a lesson plan for Lesson 5 for Lisa, and Figure 7.9 gives partial lesson plans for Lisa for Lessons 8 and 12.

Figure 7.8. Lesson Plan for Lisa—Lesson 5

LESSON COMPONENT	STRATEGIES AND ACTIVITIES	OUTCOMES AND FORMATIVE ASSESSMENT
Reading familiar text for fluency **Text:** *Animal Poems*, Worth, 2007	Lisa likes these animal poems and has become better at reading them with expression.	Read two poems with good expression. She needed a prompt on the words *buoyant* and *surly*. Do this again, but preview words that might cause difficulty.
Guided reading: **Text:** *Ocean Pollution*, Parsons, 2005 **Level:** M	**Use of text features:** Scaffold using the features she knows to make meaning (next lesson after modeling)	Lisa was able to use sidebars, captions, and diagrams to comprehend when I drew her attention to them. Created some annotations on post-it notes. Needs practice to achieve independence.
Word study: Vocabulary Semantic feature analysis on types of pollution: *acid rain, oil spills, chemicals, agricultural run-off, animal waste, garbage*	Help her use the Internet to find examples of each. Create an SFA for defining characteristics. (May have to continue tomorrow).	This was hard for both of us. I needed to do it myself before asking her to do it. We will continue it tomorrow.
Comprehension: DRTA **Text:** *Dracula's Daughter*, Hoffman, 2006 **Level:** N	Scaffold DRTA by sharing predictions.	Lisa likes *Yellow Banana* books. Stopping to make predictions helped her keep track of what was happening. She was able to make some predictions using evidence after I modeled how to do this for her. Keep working with this text using this strategy.

Lesson Component	Strategies and Activities	Outcomes and Formative Assessment
Writing Create a paragraph on pollution for the *Summer Reader* magazine	Share the pencil using her annotations. Go back in the text to expand on information that might be missing.	Sharing the pencil was a good idea. It enabled me to guide her writing. We did not finish. Continue this to completion, and then let her take more control on the next piece of writing.

Figure 7.9. Partial Lesson Plan for Lisa

Lesson Component	Strategies and Activities	Outcomes and Formative Assessment
Lesson 8		
Guided Reading: **Text:** *Oil Spills*, Parsons, 2005	Ask Lisa to use the text features to guide her silent reading. Monitor and scaffold where needed. Have her make annotations of important information.	This text is written by the same author as *Ocean Pollution* so has similar structures. Lisa is much more confident with her comprehension but does not always identify the most important information. Work on identifying the most important information.
Comprehension: DRTA **Text:** *The Monster Underground*, Cross, 2002 **Level:** N	Try having her choose where to stop. Focus on finding where the evidence is in the text. Model as needed.	I had to ask her to stop and make a prediction, or she would have kept reading. She used evidence when asked why she had made the prediction. Needs more practice to do this independently. The text is at her level.
Guided Reading: **Text:** *Looking After Our World*, Halliday, 2006 Read orally.	Introduce three important words. Lisa is getting bored with using text features, and she still struggles with coming up with a good summary. I have not tried this activity before, so we will both be learning together.	This fit well with the annotations we were doing, and she found it easier to identify important words. We did not get to write a summary yet. Use important words to write a summary.

(continued)

Figure 7.9. Partial Lesson Plan for Lisa (*continued*)

Lesson Component	Strategies and Activities	Outcomes and Formative Assessment
Lesson 12		
Comprehension: DRTA **Text:** *Rapunzel,* Zelinksy, 2002 Read silently.	This is quite a complex text, but it is a picture book, so it may be motivating for her. I'd like her to continue to monitor her own comprehension. I will stop her at unexpected times and ask her what she is thinking.	Lisa was very motivated to read this book, despite the complex text. At one point she had not really understood what had occurred, so I read the page aloud, and she made a good prediction. Still needs to work on monitoring her understanding.

Things to Think About

1. How do you use questioning in your tutoring? What types of questions do you ask for different texts? Are your students able to recognize that you are asking them to think differently and to use their prior knowledge in different ways?
2. Try using a think-aloud checksheet with your students in relation to strategies you have taught them. Did it help them with their thinking metacognitively? Did it help you refine your instruction?
3. How do you annotate texts when you are reading? Are you comfortable with this method as a means for learning? Would your students be able to use your system, or should they try one of the ideas from this chapter?

8 Writing and Reading Connections

Marcus was an 8th-grade student in a K–8 urban area where 96% of student population is classified as low-income. Marcus enjoyed reading and was especially motivated by his interests in basketball and tattoos. His strength was oral reading. Marcus had adequate reading comprehension but did not meet standards in the writing response-to-reading portion of the state test. His classroom teacher described Marcus as a motivated student who tried his best but often "shuts down" when asked to summarize or respond to what he has read. Marcus rarely completed written assignments, and to avoid writing, he often came late to class, spent time in the bathroom, or put his head down on his desk. His teacher had tried to encourage him, including meeting with his family and having him stay after school to "catch up."

In spite of all the teacher's efforts, Marcus continued to struggle. His teacher requested that Marcus receive tutoring services with a focus on writing, which was granted. Prior to Marcus's first tutoring session, Dwayne, his tutor, reviewed Marcus's assessments and administered a reading/writing interest survey. Upon review of the survey, formative and summative assessment, and the teacher tutoring request, Dwayne was not surprised by the results. Marcus did not enjoy writing, especially when the writing was about reading and required him to read long pieces of text. When asked why he did not like writing, he responded:

"Because my teacher really don't care what I wrote. She tells me to write more. I have nothing more to say—I write as much as I needed to write, and then I get a bad grade. It just doesn't make sense. Why does she ask me to tell what I think about what I read and then I'm told I'm wrong ... it's my idea, so why am I wrong? ... I never get to write about what I want to write about. My teacher tells me the topic, and I don't know anything about it. I never get it right, so why bother?"

Writing provides students with a voice. The importance of being heard through conversation and writing is especially important to school success. Reluctant, struggling writers often remain silent, putting them at a disadvantage in comparison to their peers. One of the key goals for struggling writers is to help them take ownership of their writing. Struggling writers need effective instruction, yet it is equally important to pay attention to students' attitudes toward writing, as it involves their mastery of specific writing skills.

Writing instruction that focuses on the writer gives students power as readers, thinkers, and composers of meaning (Calkins, 1994). Leading researchers and educators concur that students need to do the following:

- Choose their own topics
- Have regular response to their writing from both teachers and peers
- Write a minimum of three out of five days a week
- Publish by sharing, collecting, or posting their work
- Hear their teacher "think aloud" when modeling writing
- Maintain collections of their work to establish a writing history. (Calkins, 2012)

The same principles are true when working with struggling and/or reluctant writers.

Although the fundamentals have stayed the same over the past decade, writing instruction has lagged behind reading instruction in depth and scope. Calkins (2012) points out that the release of the Common Core State Standards (CCSS) has resulted in a resurgence of writing in the Reading/Language Arts curriculum, and has provided us with a framework for writing instruction. As cited in the CCSS Initiative College and Career Readiness Anchor Standards for Writing by the National Governors Association, students need to learn to use writing as a way of offering and supporting opinions, demonstrating understanding of the subjects they are studying, and conveying real and imagined experiences and events.

This chapter describes methods for guiding and supporting reluctant writers, first addressing: (1) the craft of writing, which addresses writing standards broadly categorized as: text types and purpose, production and distribution of writing and conventions of standard English; and (2) reading–writing relationships, which address the writing standard categorized as "range of writing." The strategies that address each of these categories can be seen in Figure 8.1, although each strategy may address more than one standard. The chapter closes with "writing to learn" activities.

Figure 8.1. Matrix of Activities Linked to Common Core State Writing Standards

Anchor Standards: Language

SL.2   Demonstrate command of the conventions of standard English capitalization, punctuation, and spelling when writing.

Anchor Standards: Writing

Types and Purposes

Write arguments to support claims ... using valid reasoning and relevant and sufficient evidence.

Write informative/explanatory texts to examine and convey complex ideas and information clearly and accurately through .... organization, and analysis of content.

Write narratives to develop real or imagined experiences or events using effective technique, well-chosen details and well-structured event sequences.

Production and Distribution of Writing

Produce clear and coherent writing in which the development, organization, and style are appropriate to task, purpose, and audience.

Develop and strengthen writing as needed by planning, revising, editing, rewriting, or trying a new approach.

Range of Writing

W.10   Write routinely over extended timeframes (time for research, reflection, and revision) and shorter time frames (a single sitting or a day or two) for a range of tasks, purposes, and audiences.

FOCUS	ACTIVITY	EXAMPLE STANDARDS*
Write opinion/ arguments to support claims Link opinion to reasons using words and phrases	Model and mentor text E I E I Oh Language frames	Grade 4 W.4.1a Introduce a topic or text clearly, state an opinion, and create an organizational structure in which related ideas are grouped to support the writer's purpose Grade 3 W.3.1.b Provide reasons that support the opinion. Grade 5 W.5.1.b Provide logically ordered reasons that are supported by facts and details. Grade 7 W 7.1a Introduce claim(s), acknowledge alternate or opposing claims, and organize the reasons and evidence logically.

(continued)

Figure 8.1. Matrix of Activities Linked to Common Core State Writing Standards *(continued)*

FOCUS	ACTIVITY	EXAMPLE STANDARDS*
Write informative texts to explain	Write like an author All about books Boxes and bullets	Grade 2 W.2.2 Write Informative/explanatory texts in which students introduce a topic, use facts and definitions to develop points, and provide a concluding statement or section. Grade 3 W.3.2a Introduce a topic and group related information together; include illustrations when useful to aiding comprehension.
Narrative to develop real or imagined experiences	Writer's notebooks Narrative graphic organizers • Story map • Timeline • Plot diagram	Grade 1 W.1.3 Write narratives to recount two or more appropriately sequenced events, include some details regarding what happened, use temporal words to signal event order, and provide some sense of closure. Grade 6.W.6.3e Provide a conclusion that follows from the narrated experiences or events.
Forms fits purpose, audience	Reading response notebooks Written conversations Collaborative writing RAFT	W.6.4 Produce clear and coherent writing in which the development, organization, and style are appropriate to task, purpose, and audience. (Grade-specific expectations for writing types are defined in standards 1–3 above.)
Editing, capitalization, punctuation, and spelling when writing	COPS Editing checklist	Grades 1–5 W.5 With guidance and support from peers and adults, develop and strengthen writing as needed by planning, revising, editing, rewriting, or trying a new approach. (Editing for conventions should demonstrate command of language standards 1–3 up to and including grade 5 here.)
Range of writing	Writing to learn Start-up and warm-up Brainstorming List/list-storming Fact/value lists Literature conversations	Grade 4–8 W.10 Routinely over extended timeframes (time for research, reflection, and revision) and shorter timeframes (a single sitting or a day or two) for a range of discipline-specific tasks, purposes, and audiences.

Focus	Activity	Example Standards*
Demonstrate command of the conventions of standard English capitalization, punctuation, and spelling when writing. CCSS.ELA 1.2	Editing checklist COPS	Grades 1–3 L.2 Demonstrate command of the conventions of standard English capitalization, punctuation, and spelling when writing.
		Grades 4–8 L.2 Demonstrate command of the conventions of standard English capitalization, punctuation, and spelling when writing.
		Grades 4–8 .2 Use punctuation (commas, parentheses, dashes) to set off nonrestrictive/parenthetical elements.*
		Grades 4–8 Spell correctly.

*Example grade level standards are from the standards for literature and for informational text.

The matrix is meant to show possible connections. Many activities apply to more than one standard. Each example represents the main focus of that standard. For example, Reading Standard 2 addresses determining central ideas or themes and summarizing.

Marcus's profile represents one type of writer who needs instruction. As is true with all students, struggling writers have different needs and will benefit from instruction that recognizes these differences.

THE CRAFT OF WRITING

Writing is often defined as a craft. There are rules that writers follow to turn out a piece of writing, whether it is a narrative, argumentative, or informational piece (Calkins, 2012). Skill is required to construct, word-by-word and sentence-by-sentence, something meaningful that others will read for enjoyment or to gain information. But while it is a craft, it is also an art. Words are chosen and sentences are arranged to keep the reader's interest. Accomplished writers continue to work at mastering both the art and the craft of writing, and in doing so, serve as models for student writers (Graves, 1994). Dorfman and Cappelli (2007, 2009) recommend mentor texts as useful in helping students learn to write well. In tutoring, mentor texts have provided excellent models for struggling writers. Following is a discussion of the craft of writing narrative, argumentative, and informational essays, as well as editing students' work.

Narrative Writing

When working with a reluctant writer, tutors begin with personal narrative. Our belief is that everyone has a story to be told, and when students write about something that is important to them, it builds their enthusiasm and engagement. The power of writing personal narratives allows students to use words that show and, tell a clear sequence of events. Students develop and strengthen their writing by planning, revising, and editing. Writing narratives that produce clear and coherent writing with purpose and audience is also an expectation of the CCSS (Fredricksen, Wilhelm, & Smith, 2012). A myriad of writing strategies are available to support narrative writing. Following are just a few that tutors have found to be highly effective when working with struggling reluctant writers.

Writer's notebook. A writer's notebook provides an easy, informal, nonthreatening place to begin writing. During each tutoring session, students write about topics of their choosing in their writer's notebooks. After they have several entries, they choose one to develop further. This is quite effective in completing a narrative piece of writing.

Dwayne was aware of Marcus's indifference to writing. He presented Marcus with a writer's notebook, explained the procedure, and expected things to go smoothly. Marcus thanked him for the writing notebook, opened it, and wrote "A Bad Day," then added two sentences referencing his bad day.

That night Dwayne reflected on the tutoring session:

> The writing didn't go as I had planned. Marcus was delighted with the notebook and choice of topic; however, he wrote only two sentences. It is just the first day, so I need to give this a chance. AT LEAST he wrote something. The goal is to have Marcus write several entries, then choose one to revise and edit. Tomorrow I plan to write along with Marcus.

Julia, a 2nd-grade student, wanted to write a book about her life. She began by listing events from her life but had difficulty choosing, then organizing the events in a logical manner. Sarah, Julia's tutor, suggested that she choose one event from each year of her life and place it on a timeline from birth to 8 years old. This provided Sarah the visual and organization support that was needed to begin the writing.

Following the fifth day of tutoring, Dwayne was impressed with the progress that Marcus had made and then decided that tomorrow would be the day to choose one piece to develop further. Use of the writer's notebook provided the support that Marcus needed to build his confidence as a writer.

Narrative graphic organizers. Many students' personal narratives lack organization. Narrative graphic organizers such as story maps and timelines help students logically organize the events in a story.

For struggling older students with difficulty in including all compo nents of a narrative piece of writing—exposition, rising action, climax, falling action, resolution—the plot diagram in Figure 8.2 is useful and a favorite among tutors and students.

Figure 8.2. The Witch's Hat Narrative Planner

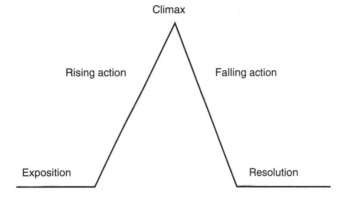

The witch's hat diagram for short stories and novels.

Argumentative Writing

The CCSS states that opinion or argumentative pieces should be written in a manner that appeals to the audience, makes a claim, and supports the claim with evidence that differs from the traditional persuasive piece of writing. Numerous writing strategies support opinion and argumentative writing (Hillocks, 2011; Smith et al., 2012).

Model and mentor texts. To establish a purpose and choose a topic that is worth the argument, tutors use persuasive/opinion/argumentative texts found in newspapers, magazine articles, advertisements, petitions, and brochures to support their point of view (Duke, Caughlan, Juzwik, & Martin, 2012). The following is an example of how a meaningful topic, supportive tutor, and mentor texts can change a student's writing disposition.

Pablo, a 7th-grade student, was a struggling writer who showed little or no interest in reading or writing. Prior to the first tutoring session, Suzanne, Pablo's tutor, chose a variety of adolescent literature, nonfiction texts, and magazines and spread them out on a table. She observed as Pablo rifled through the materials and suggested that he continue to look for something of interest. Pablo obliged and continued to search for the ideal book or magazine. He gravitated toward articles and text on Mexican immigration. As Pablo leafed through the materials, he continued to share his experiences with Suzanne. He had marched in the Chicago rallies and also went to Washington, D.C. with his family.

The next day, Suzanne arrived with newspaper articles containing narrative and expository text on Mexican immigration. Pablo began his inquiry by using the skim-and-scan comprehension strategy as he read and reread the March 28, 2006, *Scholastic News*-featured article "Immigration Protests," authored by Tiffany Chaparro, and used them as models for argumentative writing with a focus on point of view. Pablo seamlessly moved to argumentative writing, as demonstrated in his contribution (Figure 8.3) to the summer tutoring newspaper publication.

Figure 8.3. Pablo's Writing for the Newspaper (July, 2006)
MEXICAN IMMIGRATION
Background Information

Mexicans are immigrating to the United States because of economic problems. There is a trade agreement between the United States, Mexico, and Canada. The reason the Mexicans are immigrating to the U.S. is because the U.S. sells goods to Mexico for real cheap. People who had farms in Mexico do not make much money. Now the Mexicans are running out of jobs. I believe the trading should stop if the U.S. doesn't want any more immigrants. I believe the immigrants who have been living in the U.S. for at least 10 years should become legal citizens.

Do you agree or disagree with President Bush's guest-worker Program?

The guest-worker program is a work permit that lets immigrants work in the U.S. for 3 years. This is President Bush's proposal, but people in his party don't all agree. The President believes the United States will then know whom they are letting in. I agree with this program because it will give immigrants jobs and a better life. I disagree because once the work permit is over, the immigrants aren't going to have jobs or money. I believe they should allow the guest-worker program to last a lifetime.

The question I still wonder about is:

What happens to the immigrants after the 3 years?

Pablo found his voice in the tutoring program. Once a student who "hated writing" and tolerated reading, he became a highly motivated student whose disposition changed dramatically toward nonfiction reading and opinion writing.

The C-E-I-E-I-E-I-Oh Strategy. When writing opinion pieces, students are asked to make a claim and to support that claim with evidence and reasoning. Tutors have adapted the reader response E-I-E-I-O to C-E-I-E-I-E-I-O-Oh as a way to provide guidance and structure when writing an opinion piece:

C   Make a claim.
E   Evidence—support your opinion with evidence from text.
I   Interpretation—explain your reasoning.
E   Evidence—support your opinion with evidence from text.
I   Interpretation—explain your reasoning.
E   Evidence—support your opinion with evidence from text.
I   Interpretation—explain your reasoning.
O   Oh! Your voice explains why you believe this—state your opinion.

Tutors often provide language stems to support students in writing an opinion piece (see Figure 8.4 for examples).

Figure 8.4. Language Frames for Opinion Writing

OPINION WRITING	LANGUAGE STEM	
Topic sentence (claim)	My opinion is _____	
Evidence (support opinion/claim)	In the story,	the author says
	In the text,	the text states
Interpretation (your opinion/your voice)	I know	This means to me
	I believe	It is clear to me
	I think	This shows me
Oh (what was learned)	I learned	
	I believe	

Writing Informative/Explanatory Texts

As required by the CCSS, students are to write informative/explanatory texts to examine a topic and convey ideas and information accurately. Further, students are expected to write informational texts that develop a topic and link across categories of information, using precise language and domain-specific language.

Informational texts are written for the purpose of conveying information to an interested audience and must be written in an organized manner, in which facts and ideas support the topic (Duke et al., 2012). Tutors focus on teaching the structure of nonfiction texts, then move on to researching a topic.

Write like an author. Have students examine various styles of informational texts to see the structures used in nonfiction writing. Use materials that are specific to one topic, and read these together. Have students mark with a post-it the structures they notice, and discuss each of them together. This encourages students to use these same structures when writing their own informational texts. This is often paired with the reading portion of the tutoring session.

Boxes and bullets. The boxes and bullets organization is an effective way for older struggling writers to frame an essay. It is adapted for tutoring from Calkins and colleagues (2013). The boxes and bullets prewriting strategy is similar to an outline that organizes thinking prior to writing. The tutor explains to students the importance of developing the main idea around a topic they are studying, and writing it as a "thesis statement." Once the students have a main idea, they think of reasons that support the thesis statement, and each of these becomes a separate paragraph. Tutors have found that the boxes and bullet graphic organizer shown in Figure 8.5 provides the structure for a cohesive essay. Additional graphic organizers may be found at http://newarkexcels.org/wpcontent/uploads/2012/11/Graphic-Organizers-Nonfiction-5-31-11.pdf

Figure 8.5. Boxes and Bullets

THESIS STATEMENT
• Supporting Detail (Paragraph)
• Supporting Detail (Paragraph)
• Supporting Detail (Paragraph)

Editing

CCSS Language Anchor Standard 2 states that students are expected to "demonstrate command of the conventions of standard English capitalization, punctuation, and spelling when writing." Tutors have found the use of editing post-it notes as flags for proofreading edits, checklists, and the COPS editing strategy to be effective when working with struggling writers.

Editing strategies for primary students. For primary students, editing is often overwhelming. Lily's tutor Dayna wanted to provide Lily, a 2nd-grade student, with an editing checklist. At first Dayna considered having Lily work on all aspects of editing, but then realized that would be overwhelming. Dayna prioritized Lily's needs and developed a checklist with a focus on punctuation (see Figure 8.6).

Figure 8.6. Editing Checklist for Lily

FOLLOW THE CLUES

Read aloud.

As you read, listen to your voice. Add punctuation so the reader will "hear" what you have written.

Period	.	My voice stops
Question mark	?	My voice goes up a little
Exclamation mark	!	I read in an excited voice
Comma	,	I pause a little

COPS. The COPS editing strategy assists students in editing their own writing. This often is used with elementary-school and middle-school students. COPS focuses on different aspects, helping students to look for errors as they work through the editing process. Students are to reread their composition four times, each time concentrating on one of the four points in COPS:

1. **Capitalization:** Are the first words in each sentence, as well as the proper names, capitalized?
2. **Overall:** How is the overall appearance and readability (spacing, legibility, indentation of paragraphs, neatness, complete sentences, etc.)?
3. **Punctuation:** Is the punctuation correct?
4. **Spelling:** Are the words spelled correctly?

READING–WRITING RELATIONSHIPS

In the tutoring session, we have found combining reading and writing helps students develop a clear understanding of the text and written response. The connection between reading and writing should be made explicit to the students and be taught in meaningful contexts. Following are several effective strategies that we have found effective in developing the reading and writing relationship in the tutoring setting (Angellio, 2003).

Reading Response Notebooks

Reading response notebooks are used for responding to reading through writing: to record feelings, reactions, and questions about what was read. This type of writing supports the student's higher-order thinking skills. Teachers can assess students' reading and writing behaviors and use this information

Julio, a 3rd-grader, had written reading responses that often were grammatically incorrect or consisted of partial sentences. Clarissa, his tutor, recognized that Julio "needed to work on sentence structure." The following day, Clarissa redirected his writing by providing the following sentence frames: I would like to go to _____ because _(reason one)_ and _(reason two)_. I would like to see _____ because _____. The open-ended sentence frames were placed on his tutoring board for future reference. Initially, Julio referred to the sentence frames to support his writing. Clarissa noted that as Julio became more aware of sentence structure, he rarely referenced the posted sentence frames.

to determine what guidance or additional instruction is needed.

When implemented in a tutoring setting, tutors model using a think-aloud procedure in which the tutor wonders/reflects aloud while writing in the notebook. Effective tutors often scaffold writing by gradually releasing responsibility to the student, where the tutor models the writing (I Do. You Watch), then completes it with the student (We Do), helps as the student tries it alone (You Do. I Watch), and finally releases it to the student to write independently (You Do).

A variety of language frames can be used as scaffolds to support students' written responses. When introducing a reading response, provide language stems that support the student's first efforts (see Figure 8.7).

Figure 8.7. Language Stems for Reader Response

Reading Response	Stems to Be Used in Written Response
Respond emotionally Write what you liked or disliked about the book	When I read _____, it made me feel _____ because _____.
The main event Tell which event is most important. Find words in the text as support.	I think this is really about _____. I think this because in the text, it said _____.
Make interpretations What is the author saying?	The author (article) stated _____. I agree that _____ but _____. I would have to disagree with _____ because _____.

Character study Tell what you noticed about the characters. Choose words from the story that best describe the character.	When I read _____ I noticed that [put character's name here] did _____. I think [character's name] did this because _____. OR I wonder why _____ did this. I agree/disagree with what _____ did because _____.
Character study Tell what you noticed about the characters. Choose words from the story that best describe the character.	When I read _____. I heard _____. I smelled _____. I felt _____.
Compare/contrast Compare this book to another book you have read.	When I read _____, it reminded me of _____ because _____.
Discover new learning Write about your new learning. Use information from the text to support your thinking.	When I _____, I learned _____. Now I know that _____ and understand that _____. Wow! I found it amazing that _____. I still wonder _____.
Summarizing What are the big ideas in the text? Use words and references from the story.	What happened was _____. What is really important is _____.

Reading Response Tally Sheets

Tutors found the reading response tally sheet accompanying the responses to be a scaffold that was needed (see Figure 8.8). The tally sheet is stapled into the reading response notebook. After the student has completed one of the listed written response strategies, place a tally mark next to the response strategy. Have the students continue to add tallies each time they complete the written response.

Figure 8.8. Response Tally Sheet

Ways to Respond (Grades 3–9)

_____ **Respond emotionally:** Tell what you liked or disliked about the book.

_____ **Make connections:** To yourself or another book.

_____ **Make and confirm your predictions:** Find the specific part of the text that confirmed your predictions.

_____ **The main event:** Tell which event is most important, and support with words from the text.

_____ **Make Interpretations:** What is the author saying? Find it in the text.

_____ **Character study:** Tell what you noticed about the characters. Choose words from the story that best describes the character.

_____ **Visualizing:** What do you see, hear, smell, feel when you read the story?

_____ **Compare and contrast:** Compare this book to another book you have read.

_____ **Summarizing:** What are the big ideas in the text? Use words and references to support your thinking.

WRITING TO LEARN

Certain writing activities can help students to engage and explore subject matter. The "writing-to-learn" activities, across many subject areas, help the student move beyond the content of the curriculum (Marzano, 2012). The following are writing-to-learn activities that tutors have used successfully.

Start-Up or Warm-Up

Set aside the first 3 to 5 minutes of the tutoring session for the student to do a "quick write" on a topic of choice or one that was aligned to the day's tutoring lesson. This can be in the form of a question, a response to a quote, or something that was read the previous day. Having clear expectations and an allocated time frame is comforting to both the tutor and the student. Tutors find this to be an effective way to begin the tutoring session and build writing fluency, especially with reluctant writers. Two writing startup strategies that tutors have found to be valuable are listing/list-storming and the fact/value lists.

Listing/list-storming. In this written version of brainstorming, the student and the tutor each make an individual list of words or phrases reflecting whatever they know or think they know about a given subject or topic. They then compare their lists, discuss them, and use them for quick writes.

Fact/value lists. When introducing a new topic with strong values, the student and the tutor each complete a two-column paper in which Column 1 is titled "Fact" and Column 2 is titled "Opinion." To begin the process, the student and tutor each complete Column 1, Facts, by listing all the facts that each knows about the topic. Next, the student and the tutor each complete Column 1, Opinion, by listing attitudes, beliefs, values, and opinions on the topic. As the student and tutor continue to read about the topic, they validate their lists and explore their values. Fact/value lists offer an excellent strategy to support opinion/argumentative writing.

Literature Conversation/Dialogue Journal

By "talking" informally in writing about the content or reading, a tutor and student can have a private, written conversation. Upon completing the read-aloud portion of the tutoring session, the tutor and the student complete a written response on the reading. It is important to impress upon students that this is a "free-write" and they should write whatever they are thinking. During the next tutoring session, the tutor and the student read each other's response silently and then respond in writing. Prior to beginning the read-aloud, there should be a short discussion of the written responses.

After reading several of Marcus's reading responses, Dwayne was disheartened with the lack of depth and voice in the response. Marcus appeared to be engaged during the read-aloud, yet his responses lacked depth and the writer's voice. Dwayne decided to change from written response to dialogue journal. For the first entries, Marcus responded in his usual way—"I liked it." On the 10th day, things began to change.

Dialogue Journal Session 10

Marcus chose *The Journal of Scott Pendleton, WWII Soldier* by Walter Dean Myers (1999), aligned to 8th-grade curriculum, as the read-aloud.

Dwayne (tutor): I wonder what it's like to be a soldier in the army. It seems like it might be scary waiting around to go and fight. Do you know anyone who has fought in a war? Would you ever want to fight for your country?

Marcus (student): No, I don't know anyone in the Army, and I would fight for our country. I like war games, so I think it would be cool to join.

Dialogue Journal Session 11

Marcus: I wonder if Scott gets killed, and I bet he feels excited to go to war and have a M1 with him on his way to kill the Germans.

Dwayne: I agree! I wonder if Scott will stay alive or get killed. I hope he survives. He must feel excited, but he's probably nervous, too. I think he misses his family.

Dialogue Journal Session 12

Dwayne: I was able to picture in my head what it looked like on the beach and in the water. It seems so scary, but Scott is staying strong! Do you agree that Scott is a hero?

Marcus: Yeah. I agree, but if he gets killed, he's gonna be a goner and it won't matter if he was a hero. It won't bring him back from the dead.

Marcus's Entry Session 13

Marcus: Well, I think the soldiers made a mistake. They should have gotten under the water and then all of them shoot at the Nazis but, oh well—I hope they win.

Dwayne: It seems like it was really hard to fight back. I wish they could not have been killed. I'm glad Scott is still fighting. Let's hope they win!

Tutors have found that providing students with an audience and literature worth discussing this to be a powerful instructional strategy.

SAMPLE LESSON PLANS FOR MARCUS

Marcus was reading at the 6th-grade level. Dwayne listed the following goals for Marcus's tutoring:

1. Increase his comprehension in oral and silent reading.
2. Enable him to become a more independent silent reader by learning strategies to self-monitor his reading and add to his knowledge.
3. Help him to develop a positive disposition for writing.

Dwayne planned each tutoring session to consist of five main parts: word study, expository reading, study skills, writing, and read-alouds. The primary emphases for each session were: writing, expository reading, and study skills. (See Dwayne's lesson plans for Marcus in Figures 8.9 and 8.10.)

Figure 8.9. A Lesson Plan for Session 8 with Marcus

LESSON COMPONENT	STRATEGIES AND ACTIVITIES	OUTCOMES AND FORMATIVE ASSESSMENT
Word study: Vocabulary (10–12 mins) **Focus:** Complex Consonants Introduce 'dge,' and 'ge' words	Picture closed sort —model, prompt, pronounce, sort	Could explain pattern for closed sort. Great job explaining the pattern as he sorted. Had some difficulty pronouncing the words and using words in sentences. He uses visual clues when sorting. The 'g' sound is difficult for him (2nd-language learner) We will practice 'dge' and 'ge' one more time as echo reading of each column. Will also use words in sentences with sentence frames.
Partner/guided reading (20 minutes) PRC2 **Expository content:** Industrial Revolution **Text:** *The Industrial Revolution,* Collins, 2000 **Comprehension:** Nonfiction text features Summarize **Vocabulary:**	**Check for understanding** Read, cover, retell, reread Recheck and reread if needed **Vocabulary strategy** Review content cards Content index card	Marcus did well with vocabulary and was able to recall meaning in context. Will continue to have him complete/add vocabulary cards Utilized the "read, cover, retell, reread" strategy after each paragraph, then choose one important idea and listed it on sentence strip. Picking out important ideas through sentence strips seemed to help determine importance for him. Sorting by importance made sense, but he could not always explain his rationale for sorting. Did not need to have him recheck and reread because he was able to choose important idea when utilizing read, cover, retell and reread. However, still needs to explain how he determined importance. Will continue to work on this tomorrow through think-aloud.
Writing (10 mins) Argumentative writing—choosing a topic Quick-write on topic	**Strategy:** Quick Write	Marcus responded well to this segment of the tutoring session— voice and choice of topic within a 10-minute session works well for him. Choice of topic—Shorter school day. Will continue to build on this topic tomorrow.

(continued)

Figure 8.9. A Lesson Plan for Session 8 with Marcus *(continued)*

LESSON COMPONENT	STRATEGIES AND ACTIVITIES	OUTCOMES AND FORMATIVE ASSESSMENT
Read-Think-Aloud (10 mins) **Narrative Text:** *The Genius Files Mission Impossible*, Gurman, 2011	**Strategy:** DLTA– sticky notes Prediction— questions using academic language cues— student response full sentences & grammar focus	When Marcus referenced the language cues, he responded with full sentences and proper grammar. As he became more confident, he did not reference the language cues, spoke/ answered incomplete sentences, but made several grammatical errors. Will continue to model use of language frames and encourage him to use until it is internalized.

Figure 8.10. Part of Two Sessions with Marcus

LESSON COMPONENT	STRATEGIES AND ACTIVITIES	OUTCOMES AND FORMATIVE ASSESSMENT
Session 10		
Writing (15 mins) Argumentative writing draft 1	**Strategy:** Shorter school day topic	Marcus listed 12 reasons to support a shorter school day and will have to narrow down for the writing. Tomorrow will read editorial supporting shorter school day. Marcus will use information from the readings to assist in prioritizing his list and complete first draft.
Read-Think Aloud (10 mins) **Read-Think-Aloud** (10 minutes) Narrative text: The Journal of Scott Pendleton, WWII Soldier, Meyers, 1999	**Strategy:** Dialogue journal Model dialogue journal Complete today's entry at home	Marcus chose that I read aloud. Following the reading, we discussed the setting, characters, and initial problem that is occurring. Introduced dialogue journal to Marcus and gave him the choice of completing his response during tutoring or at home. Marcus chose to complete his response at home; as he said he needed time to think about what he wanted to write. Tomorrow we will begin the tutoring session by reading and responding to each other's first entry.

Lesson Component	Strategies and Activities	Outcomes and Formative Assessment
Session 12		
Writing/Reading connection "Save Our School" editorial E-I-E-I-E-I-Oh strategy	**Strategy:** Found evidence and supported with personal response Used planner E-I-E-I-O	Marcus read the "Save Our School" editorial and underlined evidence to support saving our school. Introduced E-I-E-I planner. Completed first E,I together. Marcus used text references and quotes and rewrote in his own words. Explained interpretation by asking what the evidence shows, means, or tells us. He had difficulty with this, so I modeled what the evidence showed us in reference to our topic sentence. Marcus understood the use of the planner and is excited to write this piece as it directly impacts his future (planning to close his neighborhood school). Tomorrow will continue to complete the planner, then Marcus will write first draft.
Read-Think-Aloud (10 mins) **Narrative text:** The Journal of Scott Pendleton, WWII Soldier, Myers, 1999	**Strategy:** Dialogue journal Tutor read aloud Begin with dialogue journal Complete today's entry at home	Began the session by reading our journals to each other. Then spent 3 minutes responding to each other. Marcus requested that I read-aloud the next chapter. Once again he chose to respond at home. His entry provided insight into the character and story. It was coherent; however, he needs to pay attention to sentence structure. Will provide optional sentence stems.

Things to Think About

1. Try using one of the reading/writing relationship strategies with your students. How does it help to refine your instruction and thinking?
2. Think of how you currently are teaching persuasive writing. How does it compare/contrast with opinion/argumentative writing as defined by the new Common Core State Standards?
3. Think of your current writing workshop. What modifications are in place for your struggling writers? What changes do you think are needed for alignment to the CCSS?

Conclusion

The Common Core State Standards undoubtedly will have an impact on the ways in which we teach reading in schools. Some students who previously might have been regarded as reading at grade level may be thought of as struggling readers. A change in school practices is not a new phenomenon and often influences the problems that readers bring to an intervention. We are old enough to remember when the Whole Language movement resulted in many more students who needed help with phonics. Conversely, an emphasis on phonics can produce students who need help with using all the cueing systems to decode. More recently, as a result of the overuse of curriculum-based measurement, we find that some students think the goal of reading is oral reading fluency, and particularly reading quickly.

This book presents some ways to work with struggling readers that have proved to be successful over time in tutoring and classroom situations. We have made connections to the Common Core State Standards when the focus of instruction clearly addresses the standards. Still, we recognize that our recommendations do not always fit easily into the standards framework, partly because much of what we do in an intervention addresses foundational skills. We want to conclude by revisiting some things that seem to us to be essential when you work with struggling readers.

The Importance of Planning and Reflecting on Students' Performance

Tutoring provides an opportunity to examine carefully what a student can and cannot do in relation to literacy, and to design interventions that address those needs in a way that encourages success and the motivation to read and write. Careful planning of a tutoring session that uses the appropriate level materials and allows students to be successful with some help from a tutor will enable students to experience success. We want to reemphasize the importance of students' being successful after experiencing failure in other settings. This can be achieved only if tutors reflect carefully on the impact of instruction, and modify their plans and lessons in consideration of students' performance. We are not advocating for testing and more testing but, rather, for the use of anecdotal records and formative assessments such as those shown in the lesson plans. Struggling readers often become wary of tests and usually fail with these in some way. Therefore, you have to include them in any testing, formal and informal, so they are aware of what you are testing, and how it will help them improve their literacy skills. Helping them understand what they are doing and why is not just a part of good teaching, it is a part of good testing.

Some Growth in Literacy Is Easily Measured; Some Is Not

Students enjoy the experience of seeing growth in their literacy abilities. The use of word banks, repeated readings, and similar strategies related to word recognition, word identification, and oral reading fluency gives them an easy barometer of success. But the abilities of comprehending and learning from text are not so easily measured, and showing students how they have grown can be difficult. For example, when you work on developing summaries with students, they often find it hard to recognize how much they have improved. In fact, sometimes when we see growth, others do not. We have learned to celebrate the small successes along with great improvements, and always try to show students how they have become better readers and writers. For us, the greatest success is when students start to enjoy literacy at whatever level, and come to view themselves as readers and writers.

Whether Teaching Groups or Individuals, We Need to Consider Each Student Individually

After working in our tutoring program, a teacher once said to us, "After tutoring Jesse, I will never view my class as a group again, but as thirty individuals." We have never forgotten that remark. Struggling readers and writers have their own ideas, their own feelings about literacy, and their own ways of coping in a school setting. To help these students, we must see what they bring to our tutoring, what we can celebrate and build upon, and how these students are similar to, and also different from, students we have worked with previously. Our experiences have taught us that we need to know multiple ways of addressing reading difficulties, and however much we think we know, there always will be individuals who will make us think more about what can be done to help struggling readers. We hope the ideas in this book will help you along the journey to becoming better tutors and teachers of literacy to those who need your help.

Children's Literature Cited

Bacon, Ron. *In My Room*. Crystal Lake, IL: Rigby, 1996.

Bednarz, Sarah, Clinton, Catherina, Hartoonian, Michael, Hernandez, Arthur, Marshall, Patricia L., & Nickell, Pat. *Discover Our Heritage: World Cultures and Geography*. Boston, MA: Houghton Mifflin, 2003.

Bonnell, Kris. *The White, White Snow*. Reading, PA: Reading Reading Books, LLC.

Brannon, M. *United States Discovering the US*. New York: Benchmark, 2007.

Brown, Marc. *Arthur's Pet Business*. New York: Scholastic, 1990.

Challen, Paul. *Volcano Alert!* New York: Crabtree, 2004. San Marcos, CA: Okapi Educational Materials, 2006.

Chaparro, Tiffany. *Immigration Protests*, New York: *Scholastic News*, March 28, 2006.

Chrismer, M. *Mars and Venus*, New York: Scholastic, 2000.

Collins, Mary. *The Industrial Revolution*, New York: Scholastic, 2000.

Cormier, Robert. President Cleveland, Who Are You? In *Best Short Stories: Introductory Level*. Blacklick, OH: Jamestown Publishers, 1998.

Cowley, Joy. *I Can Jump*. Bothell, WA: The Wright Group, 1986.

Cross, Gillian. *The Monster from Underground*. New York: Crabtree, 2000.

Cutting, Brian and Jillian. *What Am I?* Bothell, WA: The Wright Group, 1988.

Depree, Helen. *The Baseball Game*. Bothell, WA: The Wright Group, 1997.

Dickson, Shirley, McGuire, Margrit, and Shymansky, James. *Chinese Immigration*. Monterey, CA: National Geographic School Publishing, 2007.

Doyle, Malachi and Sholto, Walker. *Long Gray Norris*. New York: Crabtree, 2006.

Geiger, Beth. *Volcano!* Washington, DC: National Geographic Society, 2007.

Gurman, Dan. *The Genius Files, Mission Impossible*. New York: Harper Collins, 2011.

Halliday, Claire. *Looking After Our World*. San Marcos, CA: Okapi Educational Materials, 2006.

Hansen, Ole Steen. *Amazing Flights: The Golden Age*. New York: Crabtree, 2003.

Hoberman, Mary Ann. *You Read to Me, I'll Read to You: Very Short Scary Tales to Read Together*. New York: Little Brown, 2009.

Hoffman, Mary. *Dracula's Daughter*. New York: Crabtree, 2006.

Jacquier, Toni. *The Horrible Big Black Bug*. Crystal Lake, IL: Rigby, 2004.

Johnson, Etta. *Government and Citizenship, Symbols of the United States*, New York: Benchmark, 2007.

Johnson, David. *The Way to the Zoo: Poems About Animals*. New York: Oxford University Press USA, 1987.

Ling, Stanley. *Shipwrecks*. New York: Mondo, 2001.

Lionni, Leo. *Swimmy*. New York: Knopf, 1963.

Lobel, Arnold. *Frog and Toad are Friends*. New York: HarperCollins, 1970.

MacDonald, Fiona. *Pacal: A Maya King*. Harrington Beach, CA: Pacific Learning, 2004.

Marshall, James. *Fox on the Job.* New York: Penguin, 1988.

Myers, Walter Dean. *The Journal of Scott Pendleton, WWII Soldier.* New York: Scholastic, 1999.

Noonan, Diane. *Where is My Caterpillar?* Stevenage, UK: Badger Publishing, 1993.

O'Neill, Sarah. *Food for Animals.* San Marcos, CA: Okapi Educational Materials, 2008.

Park, Barbara. *Junie B. Jones Has a Monster Under Her Bed.* New York: Random House, 1997.

Parsons, Michelle Hyde. *Forests.* Pelham, NY: Benchmark Education Company, 2005.

Parsons, Michelle Hyde. *Ocean Pollution.* Pelham, NY: Benchmark Education Company, 2005.

Parsons, Michelle Hyde. *Oil Spills.* Pelham, NY: Benchmark Education Company, 2005.

Peppas, Lynn. *Wild Fire Alert!* New York: Crabtree, 2004.

Pigdon, Keith. *Silkworms.* Prahran, Victoria, Canada: Eleanor Curtain Publishing, 2004.

Puttock, Simon. *"Here I Am!" said Smedley.* New York: Crabtree, 2002.

Randall, Beverley, & Johnston, Dawn. *Kitten Chased a Fly.* Crystal Lake, IL: Rigby, 1998.

Randall, Beverly. *The Hermit Crab.* Crystal Lake, IL: Reed Elsevier, 1996.

Roper, Ellie. *What Do Pets Need?* Washington, DC: National Geographic Society, 2003.

Sacher, Louis. *Sideway Stories from Wayside School.* New York: Scholastic, 1978.

Simon, Seymour. *Solar System.* New York: Scholastic, 2007.

Simon, Seymour. *Venus.* New York: Scholastic, 1992.

Sloan, Peter and Sheryl. *Places.* Melbourne, Australia: MacMillan Educational, 1994.

Stevenson, Robert Louis. *Treasure Island* (graphic novel). Mankato, MN: Capstone, 2006.

Sutcliff, Rosemary. *The Minstrel and the Dragon Pup.* Somerville, MA: Candlewick Press, 1996.

Taylor-Butler, Christine. *Updated Pluto: Dwarf Planet.* New York: Scholastic, 2008.

Winrich, Ralph. *Pluto, A Dwarf Planet,* Portsmouth, NH: Raintree Heinemann, 2007.

Withers, Pam. *Daredevil Club.* Custer, WA: Orca Book Publishers, 2006.

Worth, Valerie. *Animal Poems.* New York: Farrar, Strauss, and Giroux, 2007.

Zelinsky, Paul. *Rapunzel.* New York: Puffin, 2002.

Further Resources

Chapter 1

Mesmer, H. A. E. (2008). *Tools for matching readers to texts: Research-based practices.* New York: Guilford.

Smith, F. (1987). *Joining the literacy club: Further essays into education.* Portsmouth, NH: Heinemann.

Chapter 2

Hall, L. A., Burns, L. D., & Edwards, E. C. (2011). *Empowering struggling readers: Practices for the middle grades.* New York: Guilford.

Johnson, P. (2006). *One child at a time: Making the most of your time with struggling readers, K–6.* Portland, ME: Stenhouse.

Scanlon, D. M., Anderson, K. L., & Sweeney, J. M. (2010). *Early intervention for reading difficulties: The interactive strategies approach.* New York: Guilford.

Chapter 3

Adams, M. J. (1990). *Beginning to read: Thinking and learning about print.* Cambridge, MA: MIT Press.

Bear, D. R., Invernizzi, M. R., Johnston, F., & Templeton, S. (2009). *Words their way: Letter and picture sorts for emergent spellers.* Upper Saddle River, NJ: Merrill.

Bear, D. R., Invernizzi, M. R., Templeton, S., & Johnston F. (2007). *Words their way: Word study for phonics, vocabulary, and spelling instruction* (4th ed.). New York: Prentice Hall.

Beck, I. L. (2006). *Making sense of phonics.* New York: Guilford.

Cunningham, P., & Hall, D. P. (2008). *Making Words kindergarten: 50 interactive lessons that build phonemic awareness, phonics, and spelling skills.* Boston, MA: Pearson.

Cunningham, P., Hall, D., & Heggie, T. (2001). *Making Words: Multi-level, hands-on spelling and phonics activities.* Lancaster, CA: Good Apple.

Fry, E. (2004). *Instant word practice book, grades K–3: Center activities, spelling activities, word wall ideas, and assessment.* Westminster, CA: Teacher Created Resources.

Chapter 4

Burkins, J. M., & Croft, M. M. (2010). *Preventing misguided reading.* Newark, DE: International Reading Association.

Fountas, I., & Pinnell, G.S. (2005). *Leveled books K–8: Matching texts to readers for effective teaching.* Portsmouth, NH: Heinemann.

Hasbrouck, J., & Tindal, G.A. (2006). Oral reading fluency norms: A valuable assessment tool for reading teachers. *The Reading Teacher, 24,* 219–239.

Mesmer, H.E. (2008). *Tools for matching readers to text.* New York: Guilford.

Pinnell, G. S., & Scharer, P. L. (2003). *Teaching for comprehension in reading grades K–2.* New York: Scholastic.

Rasinski, T., Blachowicz, C., & Lems, K. (Eds.). (2006). *Fluency development.* New York: Guilford.

Samuels, S. J., & Farstrup, A. E. (Eds.). (2006). *What research has to say about fluency instruction.* Newark, DE: International Reading Association.

Chapter 5

Blachowicz, C.L.Z., Fisher, P. J., Ogle, D., & Watts-Taffe, S. (2013). *Teaching academic vocabulary, K–8: Effective practices across the curriculum.* New York: Guilford.

Farstrup, A., & Samuels, S. J. (2008). *What the research has to say about vocabulary instruction.* Newark, DE: International Reading Association.

Lubliner, S. T., & Scott, J. A. (2008). *Nourishing vocabulary: Balancing words and learning.* Thousand Oaks, CA: Corwin Press.

Templeton, S., Johnston, F., Bear, D. R., & Invernizzi, M. (2010). *Vocabulary their way: Word study with middle and secondary students.* Boston, MA: Allyn & Bacon.

Chapter 6

Cloud, N., Genesee, F., & Hamayan, E. (2009). *English language learners.* Portsmouth, NH: Heinemann.

Freeman, Y., & Freeman, D. (2009). *Academic language for English language and struggling readers.* Portsmouth, NH: Heinemann.

Kress, J. (2008). *The ESL/ELL teacher's book of lists.* San Francisco, CA: Jossey-Bass.

Ogle, D. (2011). *Partnering for content literacy: PRC2 in action.* Boston, MA: Pearson.

Vogt, M., & Ecshevarria, J. (2006). *Teaching ideas for implementing the SIOP Model.* Glenview, IL: Pearson Achievement Solutions.

Chapter 7

Alvermann, D. E., Phelps, S. F., & Gillis, V. R. (2009). *Content reading and literacy: Succeeding in today's diverse classrooms* (6th ed.). Needham, MA: Allyn & Bacon.

Beck, I. L., & McKeown, M. G. (2006). *Improving comprehension with Questioning the Author: A fresh and expanded view of a powerful approach.* New York: Scholastic.

Harvey, S., & Goudvis, A. (2007). *Strategies that work: Teaching comprehension for understanding and engagement.* Portland, ME: Stenhouse.

Tovani, C., & Keene, E. O. (2000). *I Read it, but I don't get it.* Portland, ME: Stenhouse.

Vacca, R., Vacca, J. L., & Mraz, M. E. (2010). *Content area reading: Literacy and learning across the curriculum* (10th ed.). Needham, MA: Allyn & Bacon.

Chapter 8

Calkins, L. (2013). *Units of study for teaching of writing, grade by grade: A yearlong workshop, curriculum, Grades K–8,* Portsmouth, NH: Heinemann.

Cruz, C. (2008). *Reaching struggling writers.* Portsmouth, NH: Heinemann.

Dorfman, L., & Cappelli, R. (2007). *Mentor texts: Teaching writing through children's literature, K–6.* Portland, ME: Stenhouse.

Dorfman, L., & Cappelli, R. (2009). *Nonfiction mentor texts: Teaching writing through children's literature, K–6.* Portland, ME: Stenhouse.

Duke, N., Caughlan, S, Juzwik, M., & Martin, N. (2012). *Reading and writing genre with purpose in K–8 classrooms.* Portsmouth, NH: Heinemann.

Zemelman, S., Daniels, H., & Hyde, A. (2012). *Best practice: Bringing standards to life in America's classrooms.* Portsmouth, NH: Heinemann.

References

Adams, M. J. (1990). *Beginning to read: Thinking and learning about print*. Boston, MA: MIT Press

Allington, R. (2001). *What really matters for struggling readers: Designing research-based programs*. New York: Longman.

Allington, R. L. (2002). What I've learned about effective reading instruction. *Phi Delta Kappan, 83*(10), 740–747.

Angellio, J. (2003). *Writing about reading*. Portsmouth, NH: Heinemann.

Au, K. H. (1998). Social constructivism and the school literacy learning of students of diverse backgrounds. *Journal of Literacy Research, 30,* 297–319.

Beaver, J. (1997). *Developmental reading assessment*. Upper Saddle River, NJ: Pearson Learning Group.

Beck, I. L., & McKeown, M. G. (2006). *Improving comprehension with Questioning the Author: A fresh and expanded view of a powerful approach*. New York: Scholastic.

Bell, N. (1991). *Visualizing and verbalizing for language comprehension and thinking*. Paso Robles, CA: Academy of Reading Publications.

Biemiller, A. (2001). Teaching vocabulary: Early, direct, and sequential. *American Educator, 25*(1), 24–28, 47. (pp. 503–523)

Blachowicz, C.L.Z., & Fisher, P. J. (2004). Keep the "fun" in fundamental: Encouraging word awareness and incidental word learning in the classroom through word play. In J. F. Baumann & E. J. Kame'enui (Eds.), *Vocabulary instruction* (pp. 218–237). New York: Guilford Press.

Blachowicz, C.L.Z., Fisher, P. J., Ogle, D., & Watts-Taffe, S. (2013). *Teaching academic vocabulary, K–8: Effective practices across the curriculum*. New York: Guilford.

Blachowicz, C.L.Z., Obrochta, C. (2005). Vocabulary visits: Virtual field trips for content vocabulary development. *The Reading Teacher, 59,* 262–268.

Calkins, L. (1994). *The art of teaching writing*. Portsmouth, NH: Heinemann.

Calkins, L. (2012). *Pathways to common core: Accelerating achievement*. Portsmouth, NH: Heinemann.

Calkins, L. & colleagues from The Teachers College Reading and Writing Project (2013). *Units of study for teaching of writing, grade by grade: A yearlong workshop curriculum, Grades K–8*. Portsmouth, NH: Heinemann.

Carlisle, J. (2000). Awareness of the structure and meaning of morphologically complex words: Impact on reading. *Reading and Writing: An Interdisciplinary Journal, 12,* 169–190.

Clay, M. (1991). Introducing a new storybook to young readers. *The Reading Teacher, 45*(4), 264–273.

Clay, M. (1993). *Reading Recovery: A guidebook for teachers in training*. Portsmouth, NH: Heinemann.

Coiro, J., & Castek, J. (2010). Assessing the teaching and learning of language arts in a digital age. In D. Lapp & D. Fisher (Eds.), *The handbook of research on teaching the English language arts* (3rd ed., pp. 314–321). New York: Routledge.

Cole, A. D. (2006). Scaffolding beginning readers: Micro and macro cues teachers use during student oral reading. *The Reading Teacher, 59*(5), 450–459.

Cummins, J. (1979). Cognitive & academic language proficiency, linguistic interdependence, the optimum age question and some other matters. *Working Papers on Bilingualism, 19,* 121–129.

Cummins, J. (2000). *Language, power, and pedagogy: Bilingual children in the crossfire.* Tonawanda, NY: Multilingual Matters.

Cunningham, J. W., & Moore, D. W. (1986). The confused world of main idea. In J. F. Baumann (Ed.), *Teaching main idea comprehension* (pp. 1–17) Newark, DE: International Reading Association.

Cunningham, J. W., Spadoricia, S. A., Erickson, K. A., Koppenhaver, D. A., Strum, J. M., & Yoder, D. E. (2005). Investigating the instructional supportiveness of leveled texts. *Reading Research Quarterly, 40,* 410–427.

Cunningham, P. M., & Hall, D. P. (2008). *Making words first grade: 100 Hands-on lessons for phonemic awareness, phonics and spelling.* Boston: Pearson.

Cunningham, P. M., Hall, D. P., & Heggie, T. (2001a). *Making big words.* Lancaster, CA: Good Apple.

Cunningham, P. M., Hall, D. P., & Heggie, T. (2001b). *Making words: Multilevel, hands-on phonics and spelling activities.* Lancaster, CA: Good Apple.

Delpit, L. D. (1995). *Other people's children: Cultural conflict in the classroom.* New York: The New Press.

Dolch, E. W. (1948). *Problems in reading.* Champaign, IL: The Garrard Press.

Dorfman, L., & Cappelli, R. (2007). *Mentor texts: Teaching writing through children's literature, K–6.* Portland, ME: Stenhouse.

Dorfman, L., & Cappelli, R. (2009). *Nonfiction mentor texts: Teaching writing through children's literature, K–6.* Portland, ME: Stenhouse.

Duke, N. K. (2000). 3.6 minutes per day: The scarcity of informational texts in first grade. *Reading Research Quarterly, 35,* 202–224.

Duke, N., Caughlan, S., Juzwik, M., & Martin, N. (2012). *Reading and writing genre with purpose in K–8 classrooms.* Portsmouth, NH: Heinemann.

Fang, Z., & Schleppergrell, M. J. (2010). Disciplinary literacies across content areas: Supporting secondary reading through functional language analysis. *Journal of Adolescent & Adult Literacy, 53*(7), 587–597.

Fisher, P., & Polkoff, L. (March, 2003). Imagine: Visualization exercises to develop inferential comprehension. Paper presented at the Illinois Reading Council Conference, Springfield, IL.

Fountas, I., & Pinnell, G. S. (2006). *The Fountas and Pinnell leveled book list, K–8* (2006–2008 ed.). Portsmouth, NH: Heinemann.

Francis, D. J., Rivera, M., Lesaux, N. K., Kieffer, M. J., & Rivera, H. (2006). *Practical guidelines for the education of English language learners: Research-based recommendations for instructional and academic interventions.* Portsmouth, NH: Center on Instruction.

Fredricksen, J., Wilhelm, J., & Smith, M. (2012). *So, what's the story? Teaching narrative to understand ourselves, others, and the world.* Portsmouth, NH: Heinemann.

Graves, D. (1994). *A fresh look at writing*. Portsmouth, NH: Heinemann.

Graves, M. F. (2006). *The vocabulary book*. New York: Teachers College Press.

Grisham, D., & Wolsey, T. D. (2006). Recentering the middle school classroom as a vibrant learning community: Students, literacy, and technology intersect. *Journal of Adolescent & Adult Literacy, 49*, 648–660

Guthrie, J., Hoa, L. W., Wigfield, A., Tonks, S. M., Humenick, N. M., & Littles, E. (2007). Reading motivation and comprehension growth in the later elementary years. *Contemporary Educational Psychology, 32*, 282–213.

Harmon, J. M. (1998). Constructing word meanings: Strategies and perceptions of four middle school learners. *Journal of Literacy Research, 30*, 561–599.

Harris, T. L., & Hodges, R. E. (1995). *The literacy dictionary: The vocabulary of reading and writing*. Newark, DE: International Reading Association.

Harvey, S., & Goudvis, A. (2007). *Strategies that work: Teaching comprehension for understanding and engagement*. Portland, ME: Stenhouse.

Hillocks, G., Jr. (2011a). Teaching argument for critical thinking and writing: An introduction. *English Journal, 99*(6), 24–32.

Hillocks, G., Jr. (2011). *Teaching argument writing*. Portsmouth, NH: Heinemann.

Hoch, M., Bernhardt, R., Schiller, M., & Fisher, P. J. (2013). Three important words: Students choose vocabulary to build comprehension of informational text. *Illinois Reading Council Journal, 41*(3), 3–12.

Hoffman, J. (1992). Critical reading & thinking across the curriculum: Using I-charts to support learning. *Language Arts, 69*, 121–127.

Hudson, R. F., Lane, H. B., & Pullen, P.C. (2005). Reading fluency assessment and instruction: What, why and how? *The Reading Teacher, 40*, 70–75.

Jenkins, J. R., Stein, M. L., & Wysocki, K. (1984). Learning vocabulary through reading. *American Educational Research Journal, 21*, 767–787.

Johns, J., & Berglund, R. (2011). *Fluency: Differentiated interventions and progress-monitoring assessments*. Newark, DE: International Reading Association and Dubuque, IA: Kendall Hunt.

Johnson, D., & Johnson, R. (1984). Cooperative small-group learning. *Curriculum Report, 14*(1), 1–6.

Johnson, D., Johnson, R, & Smith, K. (1991a). *Active learning: Cooperation in the college classroom*. Edina, MN: Interaction Book Company.

Kieffer, M. J., & Lesaux, N. K. (2007). Breaking down words to build meaning: Morphology, vocabulary, and reading comprehension in the urban classroom. *The Reading Teacher, 61*, 134–144.

Kolencik, P. (2010). Affective and emotional factors for learning and achievement. In G. S. Goodman (Ed.), *Educational psychology reader: The art and science of how people learn* (pp. 211–222). New York: Peter Lang.

Kuhn, M., & Stahl, S. (1998). Teaching children to learn word meanings from context: A synthesis and some questions. *Journal of Literacy Research, 30*, 119–138.

Kuhn, M. R., & Stahl, S. A. (2004). Fluency: A review of developmental and remedial practices. In R. B. Ruddell & N. L. Unrau (Eds.), *Theoretical models and processes of reading* (5th ed., pp. 412–453). Newark, DE: International Reading Association.

Leu, D. J., Kinzer, C. K., Coiro, J., Castek, J., & Henry, L. A. (2013). New literacies: A dual level theory of the changing nature of literacy, instruction, and assessment. In D. E. Alvermann, N. J. Unrau, & R. B. Ruddell (Eds.). *Theoretical models and processes of reading* (6th ed., pp. 1150–1181). Newark, DE: International Reading Association.

Leu, D. J., Zawilinski, L., Castek, J., Banerjee, M., Housand, B., & Liu, Y. (2007). What is new about the new literacies of online reading comprehension? In L. Rush, J. Eakle, & A. Berger, (Eds.). *Secondary school literacy: What research reveals for classroom practices* (pp. 37–68). Urbana, IL: National Council of Teachers of English.

Maehr, M. L., & Mayer, H. A. (1997). Understanding motivation and schooling: Where we've been, where we are, where we need to go. *Educational Psychology Review, 9,* 371–409.

Marmolejo, A. (1990). The effects of vocabulary instruction with poor readers: A meta-analysis [doctoral dissertation]. Teachers College, Columbia University. Dissertation Abstracts International, 51, 03A.

Marzano, R. (2012). Art and science of teaching writing to learn. *Educational Leadership, 5*(69), 82–84.

McLaughlin, M., & Allen, M. (2009). *Guided comprehension in grades 3–8.* Newark, DE: International Reading Association.

Mesmer, H. A. (2008). *Tools for matching readers to texts: Research-based practices.* New York: Guilford.

Morris, D. (2008). *Diagnosis and correction of reading problems.* New York: Guilford.

Nagy, W. E. (2005). Why vocabulary instruction needs to be long-term and comprehensive. In E. H. Hiebert & M. L. Kamil (Eds.), *Teaching and learning vocabulary: Bringing research to practice* (pp. 27–44). Mahwah, NJ: Lawrence Erlbaum.

Nagy, W., Berninger, V. W., & Abbott, R. D. (2006). Contribution of morphology beyond phonology to literacy outcomes of upper elementary and middle-school students. *Journal of Educational Psychology, 98,* 134–147.

Nagy, W., Berninger, V. W., Abbott, R. D., Vaughan, K., & Vermeulen, K. (2003). Relationship of morphology and other language skills to literacy skills in at-risk second-grade readers and at-risk fourth-grade writers. *Journal of Educational Psychology, 95,* 730–742.

Niemiec, B., & Hess, E. (March, 2007). It's all about thinking. Paper presented at the Illinois Reading Council Conference, Springfield, IL.

Ogle, D., & Correa-Kovtun, A. (2010). Supporting English-language learners and struggling readers in content literacy with the "partner reading and content, too" routine. *Reading Teacher, 63*(7), 532–542.

Pearson, P. D., & Gallagher, M. C. (1983). The instruction of reading comprehension. *Contemporary Educational Psychology, 8,* 317–344.

Pearson, P. D., & Johnson, D. D. (1978). *Teaching reading comprehension.* New York: Holt, Rinehart, and Winston.

Powell, W. R. (1986). Teaching vocabulary through opposition. *Journal of Reading, 29,* 617–621.

Quirk, M., Schwanenfluegel, P. J., & Webb, M. (2009). A short-term longitudinal study of the relationship between motivation to read and reading fluency skill in second grade. *Journal of Literacy Research, 41,* 196–227.

Raphael, T. E. (1984). Teaching learners about sources of information for answering comprehension questions. *Journal of Reading, 27,* 303–311.

Raphael, T. E. (1986). Teaching question answer relationships, revisited. *The Reading Teacher, 39*, 516–522.

Readence, J. E., & Searfoss, L. W. (1980). Teaching strategies for vocabulary development. *English Journal, 69*, 43–46.

Reading Recovery Council of North America. (2004). *Reading Recovery book list 2004.* Worthington, OH: Author.

Rivera, M., Moughamian, A., & Francis, D. (2009). *Language development for English language learners.* Portsmouth, NH: Center on Instruction.

Samuels, S. J. (1979). The method of repeated readings. *The Reading Teacher, 32*, 403–408.

Short, K., Harste, J., & Burke, C. (1996). *Creating classrooms for authors and inquirers* (2nd ed.). Portsmouth, NH: Heinemann.

Smith, M., Wilhelm, J., & Fredricksen, J. (2012). *Oh, yeah! Putting arguments to work both in and out of school.* Portsmouth, NH: Heinemann.

Stahl, S. A. (2004). Scaly? Audacious? Debris? Salubrious? Vocabulary learning and the child with learning disabilities. *Perspectives, 30*(1), 5–12.

Stahl, S., & Fairbanks, M. (1986). The effects of vocabulary instruction. A model-based meta-analysis. *Review of Educational Research, 56*, 72–110.

Stauffer, R. G. (1969). *Directing reading maturity as a cognitive process.* New York: Harper & Row.

Valencia, S. W., & Buly, M. R. (2004). Behind test scores: What struggling readers really need. *The Reading Teacher, 57*(6), 520–531.

Vygotsky, L. S. (1987). *The collected works of L. S. Vygotsky: Volume I. Problems of general psychology* (R. W. Rieber & A. S. Carton, Eds.; N. Minick, Trans.). New York: Plenum.

Watts-Taffe, S., & Truscott, D. (2000). Using what we know about language and literacy development for ESL students in the mainstream classroom. *Language Arts, 77*, 258–265

Wells, G. (1986). *The meaning makers: Children learning language and using language to learn.* Portsmouth, NH: Heinemann.

Wilhelm, J., Smith, M., & Fredricksen, J. (2012). *Get it done! Writing and analyzing informational texts to make things happen.* Portsmouth, NH: Heinemann.

Xu, S. (2010). *Teaching English language learners.* New York: Guilford.

Yopp, R.H. & Yopp, H.K. (2007). Ten important words plus: A strategy for building word knowledge. *The Reading Teacher, 61*(2), 157–160.

Index

About the Authors

Peter J. Fisher, Ph.D., is a professor of education at National College of Education of National Louis University where he teaches graduate classes in literacy education. Peter taught in elementary and high schools in England prior to coming to the USA to complete his doctoral studies at SUNY at Buffalo. He has published numerous articles and chapters on vocabulary instruction and is coauthor of *Teaching Vocabulary in All Classrooms* (with Camille Blachowicz) and of *Teaching Academic Vocabulary K–8* (with Camille Blachowicz, Donna Ogle, and Susan Watts Taffe).

Ann Bates, Ed.D., is a literacy educator who has been a classroom teacher, reading specialist, and assistant professor of Reading and Language at National Louis University, where she directed the Reading Center reading improvement programs and designed a graduate course entitled Materials for At-Risk and Struggling Readers. Ann is co-author of *Reading Diagnosis for Teachers* and has co-authored several chapters and numerous articles in refereed publications and presented on a variety of topics at state and national conferences.

Debra J. Gurvitz, Ed.D., held the rank of Associate Professor at National College of Education of National Louis University where she taught graduate clinical reading courses. Currently she directs the NLU Chicago campus off site summer reading improvement program. Prior to joining National Louis University, she taught primary age students, mentored classroom teachers as the building literacy coach and served as the K–8 district reading specialist. Debra is a published author and respected educator who speaks at international, national and local educational conferences.

DATE DUE

COSUMNES RIVER COLLEGE LIBRARY

Overdue rates are **$.50** per day with maximum fine of $20.00 per item. Fines **Will** be charged for days the library is closed.